TALES OF
KING ROBERT THE BRUCE

TALES OF
KING ROBERT THE BRUCE

Freely Adapted from
The Brus of John Barbour (14th Century)

By TOM SCOTT

Illustrated by
EWART OAKESHOTT

23 Livingstone Place, Edinburgh EH9 1PD
Scotland
1975

SBN 903065 13 4

Printed in Scotland by
Lindsay & Co. Ltd.,
17 Blackfriars Street, Edinburgh EH1 1ND.

Contents

The Setting

EVERYBODY loves a tale, even though it be purely imaginary. How much more, therefore, should we love stories grounded in truth; for if they are well told our pleasure should be doubled, delighting in both the art of the teller and the truth of the tale. In this way truths that are good for our minds are made pleasant to our ears. Therefore, if my imagination proves adequate, I am minded to commit to paper a story that is both true and lasting, a tale sure to be remembered for the rest of time. For we like to have the deeds of the stalwart people of former times called up before the eye of imagination, through our reading, as if actually happening. And surely one ought to revere those who were wise, strong, lived lives of hardship and effort in good causes, and who won, often in strenuous battle, high honour and the rewards of courage.

King Robert of Scotland was one such, brave of heart and hand, and so was his comrade, the good Sir James Douglas – a knight so valiant in his time that his achievements and nobility were famous in many countries far from his own. I propose to write about them here, and may God help me to do it in such a manner that it tells nothing but the truth.

When King Alexander the Third was killed in 1286 (his horse plunging over a cliff in the darkness), Scotland suffered desolation from the lack of his leadership and guidance for over six years. At last the barons got together and busied themselves in choosing a king, the man with the best claim to the throne, from the royal line of Scottish kings. But, because they were a ferociously envious lot, there was great debate about who the man should be. Some wanted John Baliol, because he sprang from the line of the dead king's eldest sister. Others said the king should be the man who was nearest in the male line, though not so close in blood. They argued that no female should succeed to a kingdom unless no male equally well descended could be found: a throne was different from lower ranks, where it mattered less whether a female succeeded. Therefore this faction believed that Robert the Bruce, Earl of Carrick and Lord of Annandale, should undoubtedly be chosen as king. This Robert Bruce is not to be confused with his grandson, King Robert, who is the hero of our tales.

Because the two factions, the Baliol and the Bruce, could not resolve their quarrel, it was finally agreed that the case should be put in writing to King Edward the First of England (who had a first-rate legal mind), both parties agreeing to abide by his decision, which they trusted would be that of an honest and impartial judge. This is not as strange as it seems, for Edward had been a good friend of King Alexander, and the two countries had long been at peace. The Scots did not see the danger lowering ahead, and trusted Edward's probity and good-neighbourliness. But Edward had his own game to play.

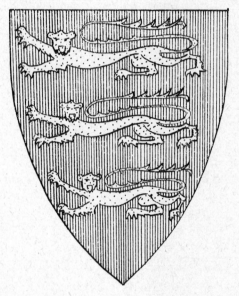

ENGLAND   Gules, 3 leopards Or.

How silly and short-sighted people can be! If the Scottish nobles had but taken thought enough and foreseen the danger, they would have acted very differently. They would have noted that Edward worked tirelessly to gain mastery by force of such countries as Ireland and Wales which bordered his own, so enslaving them that their nobles must run like foot-soldiers, or the mob, when he cried up a war. No Welshman, no matter how chivalrous a knight he might be, was allowed to straddle a horse in battle, nor stay in a castle or walled town after dark, on pain of mutilation or death. Edward held all the people he conquered in such slavish humiliation. The Scots might have realised that he would ruthlessly seize by guile what he could not reputably take by force. If they had considered the evils of thraldom and his habit of imposing it, how he took everything and gave nothing, they would have chosen themselves a king fit to rule the country without any decision by Edward. The fate of Wales should have been warning enough: happy is the man who learns by the mistakes of others, say the philosophers. Tomorrow is as vulnerable to evil as yesterday was. But, like simple, trusting people, they believed in loyalty and uprightness and had no notion of the horrors to come. Only God can have complete knowledge of such changes and happenings as will come about: for He reserves such power of foresight for Himself alone.

SCOTLAND   Or, a lion Rampant Gules within a tressure flory counter flory Gules.

The barons having made their catastrophic decision, messengers were sent at once to Edward, who was at that time waging war against the Saracens in the Holy Land. But when he heard the ambassadors from Scotland, he very quickly abandoned his other plans and returned to England: thence he wrote the Scottish barons to the effect that they should all assemble and meet him when he arrived in Scotland to fulfil their requests. His own design was quite simple – to exploit the dissension of the Scottish nobles so that, by juggling with the law, and by force, he might seize the kingdom of Scotland for himself. With this in mind he said to Robert Bruce: 'If you will swear fealty for Scotland to me, on behalf of yourself and your lineage, I will recommend you for the kingship.' But the Bruce answered: 'Sire, I swear by God that unless the kingdom is mine by right, I have no wish to be king: but if by God's will it is mine by right, then I shall hold it by that right alone, freely, giving fealty for it to no man, as becomes a king of Scotland: for so my ancestors held it before me.' Edward was furious and swore that Bruce should never have the throne. He then approached the other candidate, Baliol, and that traitor consented to become puppet under Edward's rule – from which fact came all the ensuing evil. Edward allowed him the semblance of rule for a short time, then,

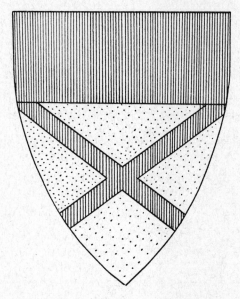

BRUCE   Or, a chief Gules, a Saltire Gules.

by legal guile and trumped-up excuses, had him arrested and stripped of all dignity and honour.

Having thus disposed of Baliol, the mighty King Edward immediately invaded Scotland and seized the whole country so completely that from Wick to the Mull of Galloway every castle and town was in his possession and crammed with Englishmen. He made Englishmen sheriffs, baillies, and every other kind of government official necessary to run the country. These officials were utterly cruel and wicked, avaricious, proud and contemptuous of anything the Scots ever did. The wives and daughters of the Scots were often violated and ill used, and if their men-folk showed their anger, the English would soon find some excuse to destroy them. They were thieves who simply stole anything that took their fancy, be it horse or hound, by hook or by crook. And if anybody stood out against their thieving ways, the English saw to it that he lived in misery, lost his land, or even his life. They murdered people as it suited them in contempt of law and order. And how cruelly they did it! They hanged good and gallant knights by the neck for little or no reason. O, how dreadful to think that a people who had always known freedom should, through bad luck and ill judgement of their nobles, have their enemies as their judicial oppressors and be so wickedly treated. Is there any greater degradation can befall man?

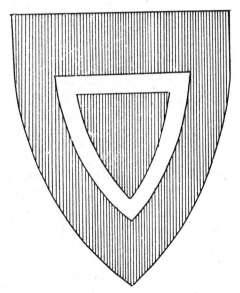

BALIOL   Gules, an Orle Argent.

O what a noble thing freedom is! Freedom gives people enjoyment in living, reasonable comfort, and he who lives free lives well. A noble heart can have no security, nor any other happiness, if it lacks freedom: for free enjoyment of life is the most desirable thing on earth. He who has never known anything but freedom may not realise what suffering and misery are coupled with vile slavery. But if he ever had to endure it, he would quickly take the lesson to heart, and attest that freedom is a greater prize than all the gold in the world. Thus do misfortunes always teach us the value of their own opposite states. The man who is a slave has nothing he can call his own, for his master, whoever he may be, owns him and his. He does not have even the negative freedom of not doing what he would not, nor doing what he would.

It is all very well for learned men to discuss whether a thrall should do first his master's bidding or first meet, if she requires it, the conjugal rights of his wife – I leave such quibbling to my betters. But the very fact that such comparison can be made, as between the rights of wedlock and the wrongs of slavelock, argues without further need of telling that slavery is intolerable. Wise men know well that marriage is the most onerous responsibility a man can take on himself: but even death is to be preferred to slavery. Death only strikes once, but slavery is a sort of living death that slowly destroys flesh,

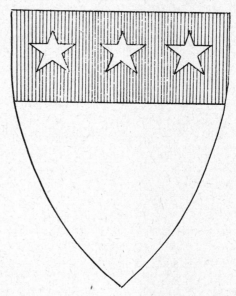

DOUGLAS   Argent, in a chief Gules 3 mullets of the Field.

blood and bone. In fact slavery is such a horrible condition of life that words fail me quite to convey the evil of it.

In such appalling slavery Scotsmen of all ranks had to exist under the English yoke. Of the nobles, some were put to death, some hanged and drawn, and others locked up in prison – and all for no real reason. Among those who were imprisoned was Sir William Douglas, father of the good Sir James. Sir William had served in the campaigns of Wallace, but had surrendered to Edward in 1297. Sir William was murdered in prison and his lands given to the Lord Clifford. Thus he became a martyr in Scotland's cause. His son was then but a small page-boy, but he became a knight of such ability that his vengeance for his father's death made his name a thing of terror among the English. He split so many skulls that nobody living can tell the number of them. But he had a very hard road to travel before he came into his proper heritage. No undertaking was too daunting for him, and he never allowed fear to prevent his doing anything he wanted to do. He was very careful always to conduct himself wisely, and he believed that no man was completely invulnerable or perfect. He set himself to achieve great things through hard toil and battles that might double his good reputation: and because of this he spent his life in great hardship and trouble. He would never

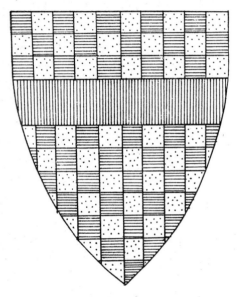

CLIFFORD   Chequy Or and Azure, a Fess Gules.

give in to misfortune but would see a thing through to the end, whatever fate by God's will befell.

When the young James Douglas heard of his father's imprisonment, and that his lands had been given to Clifford, he knew not what to say or do: for he was destitute, and none of the people he knew would do so little for him as to see him adequately provided for. Then, almost despairing, he suddenly felt the urge to travel abroad, to stay in Paris for a while, enduring his wrongs where none who knew him could see, and waiting till God should send him relief. Putting thought into action, he set out for Paris and lived there in poverty and obscurity, yet happily enough in the thoughtless pleasures of youth, often in ribald company. This was more useful to him than it would

seem, for it broadened his experience of life and conditions. Cato tells us that 'Sometimes it is wise to feign folly'.

He lived for nearly three years in Paris before word came to him that his father had been murdered. This so distressed him that he resolved to return to Scotland and do all he could to regain his stolen inheritance and redeem his dependants from slavery.

He came at once to St. Andrews, where he was very well received by the Bishop, who clothed him according to his proper rank and had him carve to him at table, wearing the Bishop's carving-knives as was customary, and appointing him to appropriate lodgings. There Douglas lived for a

considerable time, and was much liked by everybody for his nobleness. For
he was a handsome youth, wise, mannerly, and jaunty, generous and kind,
and loved loyalty above other virtues.

Loyalty should be thus prized, for through it men live righteous lives.
Given the virtue of loyalty, a man may rise high in the world: but without it,
whatever other virtues of strength or wisdom he may possess, no man will
win renown. For where loyalty is wanting, no amount of courage or manhood will suffice to get a man the reputation of innocent goodness.

James Douglas was loyal in all that he did, for he would not stoop to deal
in falsehood or treason. He set his heart on high honour, and he so conducted
himself that all who were close to him loved him. But we should not
exaggerate his good looks – he had in fact a rather sallow complexion, with
black hair, as I have heard tell. But his limbs were well made, with large
bones and broad shoulders, and his body was well built and athletic, as I have
been told by people who knew him. When he was happy, he was lovable,
and he was always gentle and unaffected in company – but those who saw
him in battle witnessed a very different side of him. He had a slight lisp
which somehow enhanced his personal charm. There are some striking
resemblances between him and Hector of Troy – the black hair, the athletic
build, the lisp, the blend of strength, wisdom, courtesy, and above all
Loyalty – though in sheer manhood and great strength Hector was in-
comparable. All the same, the Scottish knight achieved great renown for his
deeds in his own time.

Douglas lived in St. Andrews until it happened that the arrogant King
Edward came to Stirling with a great host of retainers to hold an assembly
there. Many great Scottish barons went to meet him, and among them were
the good Bishop William Lamberton of St. Andrews, accompanied by his
squire James Douglas.

The Bishop led Douglas to the King and said, 'Sire, I bring this youth here
to you. He desires to be received as your liege-man, and begs your grace to
accept his homage and restore to him his heritage.'

'What lands does he claim?' asked the King.

'Sire, so please you, he claims the lordship of Douglas in succession to his
father.'

The King was very angry and said, 'Sir Bishop, if you would keep your
fealty, make sure you never speak to me again of this matter. His father was
always one of my cruellest enemies, for which he died in my prison. He ran
counter to my majesty, so I am entitled to seize his lands. Let the boy go and
seek lands where he will, for he will certainly get none from me. The Clifford
shall keep his lands, for he has always loyally served me.'

Hearing this, the Bishop dared say no more, but left at once, being greatly afraid of Edward's cruelty. The King worked his will in Scotland and then returned to England with many powerful barons.

These were the circumstances in which the great Wallace risings took place, with what results we all know very well. Scotland was even worse off in 1306, the year in which the young Robert Bruce took up the cause, than before the Wallace rising.

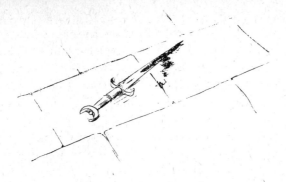

Bruce and Comyn

ROBERT BRUCE, Earl of Carrick, grandson of the original claimant to the throne, was moved to pity by the spectacle of Scotland so ruined, the people so oppressed, but had to hide his feelings till the right moment. This came when Sir John Comyn, who also had some claim to the kingship, said to Bruce as they were riding together from Stirling: 'Sir, how long are you going to ignore the way this country is misgoverned? The English murder our people and usurp their land, of which you are the rightful king. If you compact with me as follows, you will make yourself king: either you give me the lands now in your possession and I will help to make you king, or you help me to become king in return for all the lands now in my possession, so that one of us takes up the burden of the state and delivers the country from slavery. For there isn't a single man or boy in this whole country who doesn't long for freedom.'

The Lord Bruce was deeply moved by this speech, believing in its honesty, and quickly agreed. 'I will gladly take the state upon my shoulders', he said, 'for I know it is both my right and my duty – and a just cause can often make up for military insufficiency.'

The two barons thus made a pact between them, and put it in writing that very night, secured with solemn oaths and bonds.

But oh! beware of treason above all things! There is neither duke nor earl, baron nor prince, no, nor even the mightiest of kings, however wise and strong they may be, but must constantly be vigilant against treason. Was not the whole of Troy by treason delivered over to the enemy after ten years of holding out in war? Dares and Dictys, those ancient historians who knew all about it, tell us that many thousands of the Greeks had been slain in battle,

11

B

and that Troy could never have been taken by force of arms. But treason took it by guile in a single night. It is said that even Alexander the Great, conqueror of all the known world, the whole length and breadth of which he took by valour in twelve years, was poisoned in his house and his lands divided among his enemies before the last breath died on his lips. Julius Caesar also, having won by bravery in the field Britain, France, Africa, Arabia, Egypt, Syria, the whole of Europe, and for this glorious achievement was made first Roman Emperor, was stabbed to death in his own capital by his own secret council. King Arthur, too, who by his glorious deeds made Britain sovereign lady over twelve kingdoms, and who won in battle freedom for the whole of France, conquered Lucius Iberius, Emperor of Rome, was yet slain through treason and wickedness, with many a noble retainer, by his own sister's son Modred, as *The Brut* tells us.

And it was treason that ended the covenant between Bruce and Comyn, for the latter rode off to England and told King Edward all about it – though not the whole truth about it, you may be sure, for he would lie about his own perfidy. But he gave Edward the bond he had from Bruce, which was damning evidence against Robert. This inexcusable treachery later brought Comyn his own death, as we shall see.

King Edward was enraged at sight of the bond, and swore vengeance on Bruce for daring to conspire against him in such a manner. But Sir John Comyn, he said, should be highly rewarded for his loyalty: for which Comyn humbly thanked him. If Bruce, the rightful king, were out of the way, Comyn could mount the throne, and Edward would hold the whole of Scotland in his undisputed power.

But the expectations of fools, and even of wise men, don't always work out as imagined. Only God truly knows what will befall, and by His proper plan things worked out very differently from Comyn's intentions, as I shall relate.

After this, Comyn took his leave of Edward and returned to Scotland. Edward very quickly called a parliament and summoned to it all the barons of his realm: and as Bruce was at this time officially a liege of Edward, most of the Scottish lords compulsorily were, he ordered Bruce to attend it. Bruce, of course, had no knowledge of Comyn's treachery, and rode to London, where he took lodging on the day that parliament assembled. Next day, he attended parliament as bidden.

There he was called before the privy council of the King in parliament, and Edward showed him the bond he had given Comyn. Bruce realised that he was in great danger of losing his life unless he could summon up wit enough to extricate himself from the trap. He therefore took the document from Edward, who had asked him to confirm that this was indeed Bruce's seal that was on it, and looked at it carefully – or pretended to, for he was really using the occasion to think hard. Then he said to Edward, 'This will be a lesson to me – I don't always carry my seal myself, but let one of my men take charge of it. There is some knavery going on here that I don't yet understand, and to that end must consult the man who was carrying my seal and find out what really happened. Therefore I ask your permission to take this letter and confront him with it, and I will return tomorrow, when parliament is resumed, and give an account of the whole business before your full council. I pledge you my whole inheritance that I will do this.'

The King agreed, feeling sure that Bruce would never risk his lands in such a manner, and let him go with the letter until the next day.

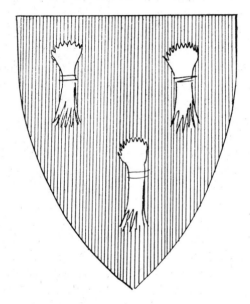

COMYN   Gules, 3 Garbs Or.

Having thus gained time, Bruce went immediately to the inn where he was lodging, greatly relieved to have been given time to make his getaway. He called his marshal to him at once and ordered him to make his men merry, as he himself would have to keep to his chamber with only his clerk, for a long time. The marshal obeyed his orders, and Bruce meantime had two horses brought secretly and swiftly to him: then he and his clerk leapt onto them un-noticed, and rode hell for leather without stopping day or night until, on the fifth day, they reached Lochmaben.

There the Bruce met with his brother, Edward Bruce, who was greatly surprised by their secret return. Robert told him the whole story, and the lucky chance of his escape from King Edward's murderous wrath.

Now it so happened that Sir John Comyn and his brother Sir Edmund were staying at Dumfries close by at this very time. Hearing this, Bruce at once rode to Dumfries to confront him with his treachery and pay him out for it. He sent a message to the unsuspecting Comyn asking him to come to a meeting in the Greyfriars church – a secret enough but unfortunate place for such a confrontation. There, before the high altar, Bruce showed Comyn the bond he had taken from Edward and, when he saw clearly the guilt in Comyn's face, stabbed him to death with a knife. Bruce's retainers also slew Sir Edmund Comyn and others of the Comyn faction. It is difficult to say what exactly happened there, and there have been many rumours about it, but all that can safely be said is that whatever happened, Comyn was slain by Bruce in the church.

Now Bruce committed a grave sin by this deed. The killing of Comyn for his treachery was inevitable and negligible, according to the ways of the times, but to kill him in a church was sacrilege, and Bruce rued it all his life. He even promised to go on a crusade against the infidel as a penance for his sin, whenever he could, and it is surprising that a man who so burdened himself at the beginning of his career should have been so successful. Yet, despite this, the Scottish bishops were among his strongest supporters, although Rome excommunicated him.

When Edward discovered Bruce's flight he was furious and swore to have him hanged and drawn – the terrible butchery he had invented for the execution of William Wallace. But James of Douglas, when word spread through the land that Bruce had risen against Edward and as rightful King of Scotland, sought and received permission from the Bishop of St. Andrews to go and join him. They met at Arickstone, at the head of Annandale, and the Bruce welcomed him and set him up with men and arms. Thus began a friendship that was never broken while they lived, and which ended in Douglas's expiation of the King's guilt for the Comyn slaying, by dying, carrying the heart of the dead King, in battle against the Saracens.

The Battle of Methven

IMMEDIATELY after receiving James Douglas into his service, the Lord Robert rode with all his men to Glasgow, where he raised many more supporters for his cause. Then they all rode to Scone in Perthshire where the Lord Robert was crowned King of Scots forthwith, in March 1306, by Bishop Lamberton of Glasgow and the Countess of Buchan. Thereafter he received the homage of many barons from all over Scotland. He knew that he would find Edward a relentless enemy and have to fight hard battles for his throne, for the English King was the fiercest, cruellest, and most unscrupulous man alive.

When Edward learned of the trick Bruce had played him, and the subsequent events, he nearly went out of his mind with rage. He summoned a knight of very high qualities, Sir Aymer de Valence, and sent him at once to Scotland with an army, under orders to burn and slay and raise the devil. The whole of Fife was offered to the man who would take Bruce dead or alive for Edward. Sir Aymer occupied Perth (Scotland was still in English hands, remember) with his men, among them such able knights as Philip of Mowbray and Ingram of Umphraville, and many Scottish knights who were still in King Edward's peace.

Bruce and his men advanced on Perth, which was defended by towered walls and battlements. Bruce was under no illusions about the quality of Sir Aymer and his knights – they were men of high ability, and although King Robert also had men of great quality, the Scots were greatly outnumbered. But though few, the Scots knights were outstandingly brave and strong – such men as the Earl of Lennox, the Earl of Athlone, Sir Edward Bruce (the King's impetuous brother), Thomas Randolph (the King's nephew, later Earl of Moray), Hugh de la Haye, Sir David Barclay, and many others – ferocious as the wild boar. James Douglas was there too, though young as yet, and others of great renown.

The Scots came in good battle order to St. Johnstoun (the old name for Perth) and challenged Sir Aymer to come out and fight. Sir Aymer at once called out his men and was about to take up the challenge when Sir Ingram cautioned him against doing so. 'Sir,' he said, 'if you take my advice you will not leave the city to fight these thoroughly prepared men, for their leader is a noble knight of his hands, both wise and able in command, and he has some sterling fighters in his company. You will be taking a great risk, for only a very great force indeed could put such men to flight: for when a company is in such good order and morale, so long as they are all true fellows ready for

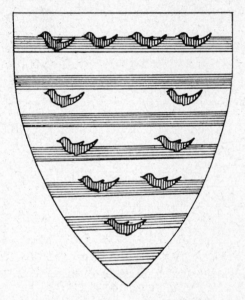

DE VALENCE   Barry of Seven, Argent and Azure, an Orle of Martlets Gules.

the fight, they have far more self-confidence than if you catch them unawares and unprepared. Therefore, sir, tell them to go back to their camp tonight and that you will fight them tomorrow – unless their courage fails them. If they accept, they will go back to camp and break ranks, take their ease or busy themselves about menial tasks, unarmed. Then we can ride out in full strength and take them by surprise preparing for sleep. They will be so taken aback that before they can recover some composure and order, we will be into the attack. Many a man brave enough in deliberate fight will go to pieces when suddenly set upon.'

Sir Ingram's advice was taken, as a result of which Bruce's men retired to the woods near Methven and set up camp. A third of them went out looking

for food, and the rest disarmed and scattered, preparing to bed down. Then Sir Aymer sallied out with all his troops and rode at full speed for Methven. The King, himself unarmed, was first to catch sight of them and give the alarm, shouting loudly to his men, 'To arms, to arms fast there, the foe is upon us!'

Swiftly they grabbed up their weapons, fastened on armour, and swiftly they leapt to the saddle. King Robert held high his royal standard for all to see, as his men rushed together, and shouted, 'Sirs, now you see how those cowards attempt by guile what they dare not try by strength. So much for our trust in the words of the English. But though they be many, God yet may give us the victory, for battles have often been won against great odds of number. Trust ye that we too conquer as they. You are knights of great valour all, and you fight for your honour. Lay on for it, then, and remember that the man slain for his country builds his castle in heaven.'

This said, they saw the foe now thundering down in battle array upon them.

Thus hastily mustered, the Scots faced the attackers. Spears couched at the ready, both sides crashed violently together so that weapons were shattered, blood burst from breast-plates; slain and sore wounded, many a man fell. Plunged strongly into the agony, eager to win glory, the best and the bravest, dealing death about them. Trampled were knights there, some bravest and best, slain and wounded, under the feet of the crowd and the horses. Blood red the grass grew, and such mighty blows of the sword-arms still in the saddle fell with strong swords that ranks wavered and broke under them. Bruce and his people manfully manifested knighthood, the King above all so hammered about him that back fell the foes from his cleaving path each where he went. So too his followers mightily laboured, blocking the ponderous onslaught of their foes. But so heavy the assault was that the Scots could not hold it, and foot over foot, stubbornly yielding, backward they staggered, giving ground more and more. Few were the King's people and nearly overcome, so that, mightily angry as he saw them falter, he uttered his war-cry in voice of iron, and so ferociously fought that all the battle trembled. Piecemeal he carved all he overtook, hammering blows as long as he could, yelling, 'On them, upon them, they falter, they fail!' And he hacked away with such vigour, while shouting, that all who saw him must count him a valiant knight.

But brave though he was and stalwart of heart, as were most of his people, nought could avail them, their followers faltered and gave way, some fled, they all scattered diversely. But still the true warriors stood ground and held battle, burning with war-rage, winning themselves honour forever.

Sir Aymer, seeing the small folk flee, one after other, and so few still fighting, gathered a body of knights and rushed boldly upon them so that he overthrew each of his foes. Sir Thomas Randolph was captured, a young unmarried man then, Sir Alexander Fraser, Sir David Barclay, Hugh de la Haye, Inchmartin, Somerville, and many another. King Robert himself was in starkest danger from Sir Philip of Mowbray, who rode bravest at him, seizing his rein and crying, 'Help, here, help – I have the newly made king!' But Christopher Seton spurred fast against Mowbray and struck him so hard that, strong man as he was, he dizzily reeled and clutched, falling, at his horse, letting go the King's bridle. Bruce raised again his war-cry and rallied his few men left there – so few, though, that no longer could they bear the brunt of the battle. Therefore they spurred horse out of the press, and the King, though sore at heart, seeing his men flee, gave in, saying, 'Sirs, as Fortune turns against us here we had best avoid further hazard till by God's grace we may soon turn the tables on them, if they pursue us.'

All were agreed, and they galloped away. But their foes too were battle weary and made no attempt to chase them, but were happy enough to return to the town with their prisoners. And so sorely they dreaded the return of the warlike King Robert that none of them dared lodge that night outside the city walls, famous for valour though they were.

They were quick to send word of their success to the King of England, who was glad to hear the news, but in his spiteful way ordered that all the prisoners were to be hanged and drawn, however many they were. This butchery was totally incompatible with the code of chivalry, and the habit of selling back prisoners for a ransom to enrich the captors. Sir Aymer therefore disobeyed the order and spared the lives of his prisoners: but he persuaded some to leave King Robert's fealty and enter into Edward's, doing homage to him for their lands, and serving his cause against Bruce. Thomas Randolph was one such. Other prisoners were held to ransom, but the most unyielding were murdered, the best and loyallest being indeed hanged and drawn – the barbarous disembowelling of a living man invented by Edward to express his rage against the great Scots hero William Wallace.

Bruce in Lorne Country

BRUCE became a hunted man after the Methven Raid, he and his men always on the run, living in the hills till their clothes were ragged and torn. They had no shoes but those they made with skins. They went to Aberdeen where they met the Queen and her ladies under the care of King Robert's young brother Neil; for the ladies were staunch in their husbands' cause. History shows that qualities of greatness, courage, endurance and loyalty may be evoked from women in adversity, and what comfort and solace they give their menfolk. But the English heard of Bruce's whereabouts and tried to surprise him with an army. Bruce had his spies and scouts, however, and was warned of the fact and that they were too many for him to risk pitched battle with, so they took to the hills again, the ladies with them. They had very little food, but the manly James Douglas saw to it that the ladies never wanted, getting them food in many ways. He hunted deer, caught pike and salmon, trout and eels, and even minnows, and also proved himself a shrewd counsellor to the King. And in this way they came to the head of the Tay.

Now in this area lived one of Bruce's deadliest enemies, the Lord of Lorne. He was the nephew of John Comyn, murdered by Bruce at Dumfries, and he planned a cruel vengeance. When he heard that the King was so near, he mustered his own men and got help from the barons of Argyll, and planned to surprise him with fully a thousand men.

Bruce was well warned of their approach, and although he had too few men with him, he nevertheless bravely awaited them. The King's men were worthy of him, and at the first skirmish they slew and felled and sorely wounded a large number of the enemy. But the men of the other side also fought fiercely on foot with axes, slaying many horses of Bruce's men, and cleaving wide wounds in their riders. James Douglas was hurt, and so was Sir Gilbert de la Haye.

Seeing his men thus dismayed, the King shouted his war-cry and charged the enemy with such force that they drove them back, overthrowing many. But when he saw that his men were in danger of serious losses from the numbers and hard-hitting of the foe, he rallied his followers and said, 'Sirs, it's foolish to go on: we have lost many horses and are like to lose many men and risk our own lives unnecessarily. So we'd best withdraw, still fighting till we are out of danger, and make for our stronghold nearby.'

This they then did in a body, but the retreat was no cowardly one, for they kept together, and the King himself defended the rear so valiantly that he rescued all the men and prevented any of the pursuers from daring to leave the main body. Those who saw his masterly rearguard defence action, turning often to face the enemy, must have realised how worthy he was to be King of a great country.

When the Lord of Lorne saw that his men were so overawed by the Bruce that they did not dare pursue him, he was furious and, marvelling that one man alone should so frustrate them, he said, 'Just as Gow MacMorn (the Fenian hero of the Ossianic poems) used to save his followers from Fingal, so this leader Bruce has saved his folk from us!'

This was a rather paltry comparison. He might more aptly have likened Bruce to Gaudifer of Larissa in the Book of Alexander, in that battle the great Duke Betys waged against the forayers of Gadres. For when Duke Betys fled from the onslaught of King Alexander and his men, Gaudifer guarded their rear with such valour and power that he brought down Alexander himself, Ptolemy, Caulus, Dauclene, and many others as well. But Gaudifer was killed at last, and here the resemblance falls down: for Bruce escaped without a scratch, having saved his whole company from the greatest danger.

Now there were two brothers in this Lorne country who had sworn to slay Bruce or die in the attempt, if they could catch him off guard. Their name was MacIndrosser ('son-of-doorward') or Durward, a family who had been among the claimants to the crown when Baliol was preferred. These bold men hated the Bruce almost as much as the Comyns did, and they had a third man to help them, a fierce and stubborn malefactor. These people saw the Bruce thus defending the retreat of his people, and they lay in ambush for him at a narrow place where he would have no room to turn his horse, but would be trapped between loch and cliff. There they fell upon him. One grabbed his bridle, but the King struck him such a sword-blow that arm flew from shoulder. Another seized Bruce's leg and tried to slip his foot from the stirrup, but the Bruce trapped his hand with his foot by standing up firmly on the stirrup, and spurred his horse forward so that the man was dragged along. Then the third sprang up on the horse behind Bruce and grabbed him so that the King was in great difficulties: but he seized the man by the neck and

dragged him over his shoulder onto the horse in front of him, and split his skull with a sword-stroke – it was an unheard-of strength. The man crashed to the ground all bloody and brain-scattered, instantly slain. Then Bruce dealt with the man still trapped in his stirrup, slaying him with the sword. Thus he delivered himself from all three of these fierce enemies.

After that the men of Lorne were terrified by the great strength and valour of the Bruce, and none of them dared attack him again. And there was a baron called MacNaughton who, so impressed and secretly admiring Bruce's great feats of arms was he, said to Lord Lorne, 'Certainly you now see retreating the mightiest warrior you have ever seen in your life. For that knight has slain in a very short time three very strong and proud men and so demoralised our troop that no man dares pursue him: and it is clear that he has no fear of us, so often he turns his horse to meet us.'

'Faith, it seems to please you that he slays our people in such a way,' replied the Lord of Lorne.

'No, sir,' said MacNaughton, 'God knows that that is not true, if I may say so. But whether a man is friend or foe, true chivalry should be admired. And certainly I have never in my whole life heard of, even in song and romance, a man who achieved so much in so short a time.'

While they were thus talking of the King, he himself rode after his men and led them to a place of safety where they need not fear their enemies. And the men of Lorne went off smarting with wounded pride.

That night the King set watch and ordered his people (for the ladies were still with them) to make merry as best they might. He told them that dejection is the worst thing possible, for it leads to despair, and despair leads to defeat: for if the heart is discouraged, the body is worthless. And he himself told them heroic tales of knights of old, to keep their spirits up, feigning a cheerfulness he was far from feeling, and fortifying their hearts.

Bruce on the Run

THERE followed a time of great trial for King Robert and his men, when they were hunted from place to place like animals. The ladies and some of the elderly men were unable to stand it, and were sent off to Kildrummy Castle under the care of Neil Bruce. It was thought that this castle was so strong that, if well provisioned, it could hardly be taken by force. It was a painful leave-taking for the King and his wife, and both women and men wept as they separated from each other. Bruce gave all his horses to the ladies and henceforth was on foot through long hardship. How sorely they suffered through winter of cold and hunger defeats description, but as the winter hardened they were driven to go to Kintyre, where they might fare better.

To get to Kintyre they had to cross the sea, and Bruce sent Sir Neil Campbell to get boats ready for the crossing, in which Sir Neil was highly successful. It was Campbell country, and the clan rallied round. Bruce made his way to the coast via Loch Lomond, where all they could find to ferry them across was a little sunken coble that James Douglas came across. It would only take three at a time, and one of each three had to row it back, so that really only two at a time could go: yet in a day and a night all were safely brought over with their baggage. The King, to while the time away, read the romance of Fierabras to those around him, and other inspiriting tales, and kept them amused till the whole company was over.

The country they had now to go through to the coast was full of their enemies, yet they kept their spirits up. But they often suffered from the acute shortage of food, and for this reason split into two parties to hunt deer, the one headed by Douglas and the other by Bruce himself. A great part of the day was spent hunting in the hills and woods, and setting snares – but they took very little to eat.

It happened that the Earl of Lennox was in the hills near them one day, and when he heard the sound of horns and the shouts of the hunters, he sent his scouts out to inquire into it, and soon discovered that it was the King and his men. Now Lennox was a man loyal to Scotland and the Crown, and, being overjoyed at the news, rode at once with his whole company to meet the Bruce. He had believed that the King was dead, having heard no more of him after the rout at Methven, and had been restlessly mourning him. Now therefore he delightedly and very humbly greeted the King, and Bruce as gladly welcomed him, kissing him tenderly, as did all the lords at that joyful meeting. It was most moving to see them weep for pity and joy at meeting friends they thought were dead, and Bruce weeping with them. But though I say it was weeping, in fact that is scarcely the term. Men hate weeping, and it is only wrung from them by extreme harrowing, though women can cry when they feel like it, whether they are hurt or not. But joy or pity can cause men to be so moved that the heart floods the eyes with what looks like tears: for true weeping in men comes from extreme pain of heart only, and this shedding of tears for pity or joy or other high emotion of the sort is not really weeping, but a manifestation of sensitiveness.

Thus by the grace of God were the barons brought together, and as the Earl of Lennox had plenty of food with him, and gave it gladly, they ate ravenously, their stomachs being so well scoured that they needed no other sauce to whet their appetite. They ate and drank all they had, and praised and thanked the Lord God that they had thus met up with their friends. The King then inquired how the Earl and his people had fared since they had last met, and listened earnestly to their stories of hardship, brave deeds and distress, deeply sympathising with their sufferings. Then he told them of his own hardships and sufferings, and his people's, and they were all moved to mutual sympathy at the recall of these past sufferings, and the telling so relieved both high and low that the experience was akin to pleasure. For there is indeed pleasure in recounting old pain and distress, once they are past, and there is no shame, dishonour or wickedness in this.

After this happy meeting, the King rose and made haste with all his company for the coast to meet up with Sir Neil Campbell, who had boats and food and all things necessary for their crossing. They embarked without any more ado, some men taking helms, some oars, and rowed via the Isle of Bute. Many a noble youth might have been seen there labouring on the rising and falling oars, sharp eyes searching the coastline, fists mightily formed for the spear-shaft now so taxed by the oars that skin was left on wood. All were busy, both knight and youth; none was spared work on steering and rowing, to further the voyage.

But by some chance for which I know not the reason, the Earl of Lennox, who was crossing with them, was left behind in his galley as the King sped far on his way. And when this was seen by certain traitors among his people left ashore, they mustered and followed him in boats, intent on taking him. The Earl saw that he did not have men enough to fight these traitors, the King's ships were too far ahead, and that there was nothing for it but to pile on all speed: but still the traitors came nearer and nearer. When they were so close that he could even hear their threats, he said to his men, 'Unless we can think of something to do about it, these men will soon overtake us. I think therefore that we should throw all we're carrying except our armour into the sea. This will not only lighten the ship and increase our speed, but they will stop to pick up the gear while we make our escape.'

This plan worked, and the Earl arrived safely in Kintyre, where he told the King all about his adventure. The King listened, but instead of congratulating Lennox on his escape and the clever ruse he made it by, the Bruce said seriously, 'Sir Earl, since you managed to make your escape we will not complain about the loss of valuable gear. But there is one thing I must say. It is of the utmost importance for troops in such conditions to keep close together and never stray far from the leader, and from the main body of the troops. I have noticed that you tend to stray somewhat from the main body, and that when you do you invariably get into trouble. Therefore I think you had best keep close to me in future.'

'Sire,' replied the Earl, 'I shall do as you say. I will in no way allow myself to be separated from you until, by the grace of God, we are strong enough to dominate the enemy.'

The Lord of Kintyre at that time was Angus of Islay, and he came into the King's peace gladly, giving him his own castle of Dunaverty for his greater safety. The Bruce thanked him greatly and welcomed him into his service, but he was necessarily always on guard against treason, and never trusted any man till he knew him thoroughly. But this wariness and vigilance he never betrayed outwardly, and he stayed in Dunaverty for three days and more.

After that he decided that he and his men should go across to Rathlin Isle, an island three-quarters across from Kintyre to Ireland, where the tide is as strong and dangerous as the Race of Brittany, or the Straits of Gibraltar. They got the ships ready and when anchors, ropes, sails, oars and other things necessary for the voyage were in order, they set out on a favouring wind. They crowded on canvas and soon were past the Mull of Kintyre and into the tide-race, where the current was so strong that wild waves rolling high as the hills were breaking on their bows.

The ships rode well on the waves, having the right wind behind them, but to an observer it must have been a frightening spectacle. At times a ship would rear up on the crest of a wave, another would plunge down as if into hell, and another rise suddenly on a wave. Great skill was needed to save their tackle in such a convoy in such seas, and often, as they neared land, they

would lose sight of the coastline among the waves, which also often hid the ships from each other.

Yet they all arrived safely at Rathlin, each thankful to have escaped the terrifying waves. They landed in proper military manner, and when the people of the island saw armed men thus arriving, they fled with their cattle towards a strong castle nearby. Women screamed and ran hither and thither with their animals, but the King's men, being swifter of foot, overtook them and brought them back. Then the King so reassured them that they all became his men and undertook to place themselves and theirs at his service. They pledged that as long as he cared to remain there, they would supply food for 300, acknowledge his lordship, on the understanding that they and their freedom and possessions were to be unmolested.

This covenant entered into, next day all the islanders knelt and did homage to the King and swore fealty and loyal service to him. And as long as he was there in the island this pact was fully honoured on both sides.

c

Death of the Hammer of the Scots

While the King was lying low in Rathlin Isle, his people were being forged into a powerful weapon for his hand by the 'Hammer of the Scots', as Edward I boasted himself to be. The persecutions they suffered at the hands of their English overlords were appalling. Severe, strict, mercilessly cruel, they spared nobody no matter what his rank, churchman or layman, whom they suspected of loyalty to King Robert. The good Bishop of Glasgow they kept loaded with fetters in a dungeon: the Bishop of Man (then a Scottish isle) they treated in exactly the same way. A vile traitor and disciple of Judas, MacNab by name (may he roast in hell for the deed!), betrayed the noble Christopher Seton, who had always treated him like a friend. The English took him straight to Edward in England, and that ruthless tyrant had him disembowelled and quartered. It is disgraceful so to treat a valorous nobleman. Sir Ranald Crauford and Sir Bryce Blair suffered a similar fate in a barn at Ayr.

Worst of all, no longer safe in Kildrummy Castle, the Queen and her entourage sought refuge in Tain, but the people of Ross betrayed her for fear of Edward, and they were all taken and transported to England, where the men were all disembowelled (the sentence included burning their entrails before their own eyes, in all such cases) and the women were sent to separate prisons, in various castles and dungeons. Sir Neil Bruce and the Earl of Atholl remained at Kildrummy to defend it, and prepared to withstand a long siege.

29

But when Edward heard of this, he was moved to one of his customary insane paroxysms of rage, and he called to him his son, Edward the Prince of Wales (so called), and the Earls of Gloucester and Hereford, and sent them to Scotland to take the castle and either slay all the defenders or bring them prisoner to him, that he might do so himself.

With a great army they marched north and laid siege to the castle; but though they made mighty assaults upon it, they were driven off by the valiant defenders. The defenders often sallied out upon their enemies, and altogether caused heavy casualties. The besiegers, in fact, despaired of taking it and thought of returning to England. But that fell monster Treason once more came to their aid. There was a treacherous scoundrel called Caborne inside the castle, and for what reason or gain I know not, this wretch (so the survivors afterwards reported) took a hot iron from a fire and threw it into the heap of corn stacked up as provision in the great hall of the castle, so that it all went up in flames.

Pride and fire, they say, cannot long be hidden, and soon the clear flame showed through the thick wooden floor, at first small as a star, then like a moon, and soon the whole floor was aglow. Then the fire burst out in great blazing conflagration, with great columns of smoke, and the whole castle was caught by fire that no human power could overcome. The defenders in the castle retreated to the walls, which were battlemented on the inside as well as the outside – a fact which undoubtedly saved their lives, for these inner battlements broke flames which would otherwise have caught them.

But when the besiegers saw the fire, they lost no time in springing to arms and attacking the castle at those places where the fire was less fierce. Yet the defenders put up such a fight that they managed to keep the enemy at bay, though at great peril. Fate, which decides all matters in this world, was against the defenders, harrying them with fire from within and enemies without – and despite their efforts the enemy burned down the castle-gate. Yet, so fierce was the heat from the fire in the castle, they dared not enter there and then, but waited for daylight.

The defenders were indeed in a bad way; yet so manfully they laboured through the night that by daylight they had again walled up the gateway. Once the sun was up, however, the enemy came again in full battle order, and the defenders, with all their supplies destroyed by the fire, made parley with the enemy and agreed to surrender themselves to Edward's mercy. This was soon shown to them – they were one and all disembowelled and quartered.

The castle once taken, the besiegers razed it almost to the ground, and began to retire to England.

Now King Edward, hearing how Neil Bruce was thwarting his son

Edward, one of the strongest knights of his day, had already mustered a great force and marched hurriedly himself to Scotland. But the old tiger was now failing rapidly, and he had no sooner reached Northumberland than he was stricken with such illness that he could neither ride nor walk. He was forced to halt at a wretched little place nearby, and even at that it was only with great trouble that his men managed to get him to it. He was so ill that he could hardly draw breath, and could only speak in whispers. But he asked the name

of the place where he lay, and was told it was called Burgh-in-the-Sand. 'Then', said he, 'my hopes are all ended. I had been forewarned by my familiar spirit that I should die at Burgh and nowhere else, but I thought it was the Burgh of Jerusalem that was meant. I thought that until I went to Jerusalem, I could not die. Now I see that my interpretation was wrong, and my death is now upon me.'

So he complained of his own folly, as he had reason to do, for he thought that he could know what no man can know – the place and time of his death.

Men said that indeed he kept a spirit which answered his questions at will, but if so, he was a fool to trust it. Such creatures hate mankind and seek to overthrow men for sheer envy, for they know that by salvation mankind will be elevated to the seats in heaven from which they themselves were hurled down for their pride. Such fiends, called up by sorcery, often give ambiguous answers to trick those who believe in their power, as in the case of the Earl Ferrand of Portugal, whose mother had dealings with Satan.

Thus it fell about with King Edward. Through sorcery he had been led to believe that he would die in Jerusalem Burgh, but instead he died at Burgh-in-the-Sand, in England.

But he did not die without some comfort to his own wicked heart and without doing his last crime against the Scots. For when his death was near, the besiegers of Kildrummy arrived with their prisoners, and told him of the fate of Kildrummy. They then asked the dying King, who should have been making his peace with God, what was his will with the prisoners. In one last rally of hate he raised his grim head and snarled at them, 'Hang and disembowel!' This utterly shocked everybody who heard him, that he, a man near to death himself, himself about to cry on the mercy of God, would show no mercy to others, and they valiant men. But as he commanded, so it was done, and the blood of that butchery was scarcely dry before the old tyrant himself died and was buried, and his son became King.

The Road Back - Brodick Castle

JAMES DOUGLAS fretted through that long winter on Rathlin Isle, and in the early spring he said to Sir Robert Boyd, 'It's not right that we should idle here battening on these poor islanders. I hear tell that in Arran the strong castle of Brodick is manned by a few score Englishmen who usurp the lordship of the island. Let us go there and see if we can do them some mischief.'

Sir Robert, who knew Arran well, agreed that they should go there secretly and lie in ambush for the English. They got the King's permission and rowed via Kintyre, making the last crossing from Kintyre to Arran after darkness had fallen. When they arrived, they drew their galley up under a hill and covered it with brushwood, the tackle, oars and rudder with it, then stole away in the darkness so that by daylight they were safely in ambush near the castle. Wet and tired though they were, they were resolved to stay there till opportunity offered.

At that time the castle was held by Sir John Hastings and a pride of knights and squires and stalwart yeomen – a fine company of men. Many a time they amused themselves hunting, and none dared oppose them. Now it happened that just the previous evening the under-warden had arrived near the place of ambush with three boats loaded with various provisions for the castle, and soon Douglas and his men saw over thirty Englishmen leave the boats loaded with various gear – wine, arms, and the like. When these men were near enough, the raiders broke cover and with all their pent-up ferocity so attacked the English, who roared like cattle in fear of death, that soon all were mercilessly slaughtered.

The uproar was heard by those in the castle, and they sallied out to help

33

their comrades, but Douglas, by the time they arrived, had rallied his victorious men and rushed furiously to meet them. At sight of these grim and vengeful men rushing to meet them, the garrison took fright and fled, chased back to the castle by their pursuers, who caught and slew many of them right in the castle gate. But those who got in barred the gate so quickly, at the expense of their own comrades, that the Scots turned back to the boats, where some Englishmen were still on guard: and when these men saw the Scots coming back, they speedily put to sea, rowing for all they were worth. But the wind was against them, raising such breakers that they could not get out to sea. They dared not try to land again but stayed there plunging about so long that two of the three boats were swamped. Seeing this, Douglas gathered up all the abandoned gear he could find and retreated, well pleased with the plunder and the morning's work. They secreted themselves at a narrow place at the head of Glen Cloy (where the earthworks of their camp can still be seen) and waited there for the King and the main company, who arrived some ten days later.

The
First Blow in Scotland-Carrick

BRUCE arrived in Arran with thirty-three small galleys, and a woman loyal to the King guided him to Douglas. Joyful was the meeting, and the news of Douglas's success. Next day, Bruce held a privy council and addressed it thus:

'You know very well how the English have driven us out of our rightful lands, and how they would destroy us all without mercy if they could. And if they did, which God forbid, there would be no recovery for Scotland. Therefore human nature urges us to action and vengeance, and three obvious principles should govern our procedure. Firstly, there is self-defence, for our enemies would not spare our lives if they got us in their power. Secondly, these enemies enjoy what is ours by no other principle than might over right. And thirdly and most importantly, there is the satisfaction that awaits us if we are victorious, as we may be, and have the strength to overcome their cruel tyranny. All these prompt us to be of good heart, letting no setback depress us, thrusting forward always towards the goal full of honour and renown. Therefore, my lords, if you are agreed on the appropriateness of this action, I shall send a man to spy out the situation on the mainland, and who is friend or foe to the Kingdom. I shall send him to my own lands of Carrick first, and if he judges that we may land there, he shall make a fire on a certain day on Turnberry Point as a signal for us to come: and if he judges it unsafe, no fire will be lit. In this way we will know whether it is safe to cross or not.'

They all agreed to this proposal, and the King chose his man well, a Carrick man called Cuthbert, in every way reliable, and briefed him thoroughly, then sent him on his mission. Now Cuthbert found much hostility and little friendship for King Robert, mainly because people were afraid of the English usurper, Sir Henry Percy, who terrorised the people from his stronghold in Turnberry Castle, where he lived with about 300 men. Seeing the people so cowed by English cruelty, Cuthbert felt unable to reveal his identity to anybody, determined against lighting the fire, and on hurrying back to advise the King how badly things were.

But back in Arran, the King on the appointed day thought he saw the fire burning at Turnberry, and his men also thought they could see it, and they

PERCY   Or, a lion Rampant Azure.

prepared at once to set sail across to the mainland. But as all was making ready, the King's hostess came to him and said privately, 'I have skill in fortune-telling, and before you go I will tell you what will become of your adventure. You do not know what awaits you in the future, but let me assure you that once you have landed no power of man will cause you to leave your country again till you have established yourself King of all the land and overcome your enemies. Great sufferings are before you, but you will triumph over each. And to prove my good faith in saying this, I will send my two sons with you to share your fortunes: and I am sure they will be properly rewarded when you come into your own high destiny.'

The King thanked her heartily for her encouraging words, but he kept his

own reservations about her words, for he was very doubtful of the powers of fortune-telling, as well he might be. For how can any man know, by means of the stars, all or part of the things to come, unless he be inspired by God? And prophets are few and far between these days, though astrologers and necromancers try by very suspect methods, more of the Devil than of God, to foresee the future.

It was a fine spring day, birds singing in the trees, the woods greening, flowers blossoming, when the King and his little fleet, about 300 men in all, set sail from Arran, late in the afternoon. They rowed hard, and after night fell they were guided only by the light of the fire, burning ever brighter as they drew nearer. Soon they were beaching their ships close to where the fire still burned. But Cuthbert, who had also seen the fire, was waiting for them full of rage and grief, not daring to put the fire out. He burst out his tale of the hostility of the countryside and of the unhappy coincidence of the fire, rousing the King's suspicion of his treachery for a moment. But this soon passed as the King saw the truth. He hurriedly held a council of war and asked what should be done. His brother Sir Edward Bruce made the first, typically impetuous answer, saying, 'No matter what the rest of you do, I for one will certainly not be driven to sea again for any danger known to humankind. Here I am and here I stay, come hell or fair weather!' And his more judicious brother the King said more soberly, 'Since you will have it so, my brother, so be it. Let us together accept whatever God sends us – weal or woe, comfort or suffering. And since it seems that Percy and his host have seized upon my heritage and are full of hate for us, I am of a mind to slake my vengeance on them. They lie unguarded here, having no reason to expect any attack from us, and even if we slew the lot in their beds we could hardly be blamed for it. So long as a soldier keeps good faith with his essential honour, he should not think too closely whether he conquers the foe by strength or guile.'

This said, they crept along to the village so soundlessly that nobody was alarmed. Then they suddenly rushed to it, stove the doors in, and slew every man they could lay hands on. The defenceless enemy made most pitiful appeals for mercy, but none was shown these agents of evil and grief, the only man to escape being the traitor MacDowal who had betrayed Bruce's two brothers, Thomas and Alexander, into Edward's power. He escaped into darkness. Percy heard the cries and tumult from the safety of the castle, but was too frightened to come out and help his henchmen in the village below. He and his men spent the night cowering fully armed while the slaughter went on down in the village. The King shared out the spoils of war among his men, and stayed in the village for three days unmolested. The English had had a foretaste of things to come from King Robert the Bruce, with this first blow struck on the mainland. Bruce stayed in Carrick for some time, sizing up the feeling of the people and learning friend from foe: but though the people were with him in spirit, they had been cowed by English terrorism and feared to show it. There also the King learned from a friendly lady of the fate of Kildrummy and its defenders, and of his women-folk. The King mourned his losses, but the pain of sorrow only hardened his resolve to be avenged on the English and free his country of their arrogant and cruel rule for ever.

The Douglas Larder

Now the Percy lay all this time in dread of King Robert, not daring to leave Turnberry Castle for the one at Ayr, which was full of Englishmen. He had sent word to his friends in Northumberland asking them to come and rescue him. They were divided among themselves about the wisdom of such a venture so far into Scotland. Sir Walter Lisle was all against it and frightened others with his imaginings of the dangers involved. But Sir Roger St. John, a knight of outstanding valour, inspired them with his forceful mind and words, so that they all set off for Turnberry. They reached the castle quite safely, with no opposition from the Scots, who were gathered elsewhere, and the jittery Percy was thankful to make his escape to England.

Young Douglas found the inactivity at Carrick too irksome for his eager temper, and one day he came to the King and said: 'Sire, I want your permission to ride into my own lands and find out what's going on and how my people are being treated. It's as much as I can bear to think of Clifford enjoying my heritage unscathed, and am determined to give him as hot a time of it as I can, while I am able to lead so little as a single peasant follower.'

'To be honest,' said the King, 'I have my doubts about such a foray into country where the English are so strong and you won't know friend from foe.'

'I have no choice, Sire,' Douglas replied. 'I simply must make contact with my own people, come what may.'

'Then go with my blessing,' said the King, 'since go you must. But if any mischance befall you, get in touch with me at once, for my heart is with you and I will hazard my fate with yours.'

The Douglas agreed to this, and reverently took leave of his lord and friend. With only a couple of yeomen he set off for Douglasdale, eager to make a start, even with so small a force. A good beginning is of the utmost importance to an enterprise, for if boldly and wisely followed up it can often snatch a victory from almost certain defeat. So it proved here, for Douglas was wise enough to use guile rather than force to attain his ends.

It was already dark when Douglas arrived in Douglasdale. He at once sent one of his men to contact a certain Thomas Dickson, an old and loyal friend of his father's and of his own boyhood, asking him to come alone and speak privately with him. Dickson came at once, and when he knew surely who Douglas was, he was overcome with emotion, and, being a substantial man rich in gear and influence, kept all three secretly in his house and saw to their needs.

While they were thus secreted, Dickson busied himself among the people, testing the loyal-hearted and dependable men, bringing them one by one to do homage to their rightful lord – which he was himself the first to do. Both in number and quality they rejoiced the heart of the young lord, who questioned them closely about the state of affairs in the county, and they told him

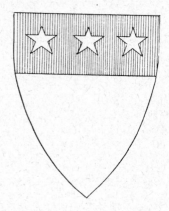

all that they knew. It was agreed that Douglas should remain in hiding until Palm Sunday, when the folk would all be assembling at the kirk. The men of the castle would be there too, carrying their palm-leaves, with no fear of any molestation. Douglas would join the worshippers with his two followers, all three disguised as peasants but wearing arms under their old cloaks. When he judged the time ripe, he was to shout his war-cry, 'A Douglas, A Douglas!' and at that signal all the loyal followers, who would also be armed, would throw off their disguises and attack the English in the middle of the kirk, so that none might escape. Then the castle would be at their mercy.

This plan accepted, they went home each to his own house, keeping the secret till the appointed day, three days ahead.

That Sunday people went as usual to St. Bride's kirk, and all the men of the castle except a cook and a porter went with them. James Douglas was in-

formed of their coming, and hurried off to the kirk. But by some silly
mistake, over-nervousness, excitement, or whatever, one of his men anti-
cipated him and cried out too soon, 'A Douglas, A Douglas!' Dickson at
once threw off his cloak and attacked the Englishmen nearby him in the
chancel, rushing valiantly among them with his sword. But he had only one
man to help him, and both were slain. Douglas himself hurried up to the
church and raised the cry again, hurling himself and his men at the now alert
and defended chancel. The fight was longer and harder than it need have been
but for that foolish cry, which had cost the good Dickson his life, but after

heavy in-fighting the Scots prevailed, killing two-thirds of their opponents and taking the rest prisoner.

Douglas, who had been the most ardent attacker in the fight, now hastened to the castle, having secured his prisoners meantime, to take it by surprise. He sent ahead of him five or six men least likely to rouse suspicion, and they, finding the gates open, went in and quickly arrested the cook and the porter. When James Douglas arrived on their heels in person, he found the tables laid for a meal, and the food already prepared, as if fate had arranged a proper welcome for the true lord of the castle at his home-coming. So Douglas and his men sat down at their ease and did full justice to this provident dinner. Then, at their leisure, they packed up all the gear they thought they could carry away, especially armour, treasure and clothes. The foodstuffs which they were unable to take away, all wheat, malt, flour, meal and such, was heaped in the wine-cellar. He then brought in all the prisoners he had taken and had them beheaded so that their blood mixed with the grain. He then had the bungs knocked out of the huge tuns of wine, soaking the whole into an unearthly foul mixture of blood, flour, wine and all. This grisly concoction was known among the folk for years after as 'the Douglas Larder'. Douglas could not at that time have held the castle, you see, and therefore he was using that 'scorched-earth' policy which marked the whole of the Scottish Wars of Independence, as it was later to mark many another strategy in other parts of the world.

The dead horses were then slung in the well to foul it, along with all the salt; the castle was put to the flame, and with a heavy heart Douglas abandoned it to its fate. Without enough food supplies, men, or hope of rescue, it would have been quite impossible to defend it, and wasteful and dangerous to try. 'In such circumstances', he said, 'it is better to hear the lark sing than the mouse squeak.'

Thus was young Douglas's homecoming a thing of both triumph and grief. Douglas and his men then scattered into hiding or to their own homes and comparative safety among the people. The wounded were tended secretly until they were well again, for the English were still in power throughout the whole of Scotland. Clifford was furious when he heard the news of the Douglas Larder, and went at once to the castle and had it rebuilt and strongly garrisoned, with one of the Thirlwall family as captain in charge.

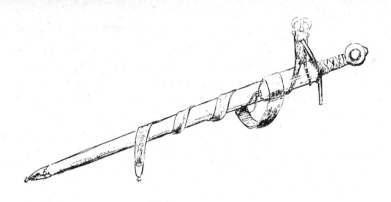

Bruce and Three Traitors

DURING Douglas's absence the King stayed in Carrick with a handful of men, not more than 200, while his brother Sir Edward went foraying in Galloway with the others. They dared not ride about openly as yet, so they kept to less accessible fastnesses.

Now Sir Aymer de Valence, the English Warden of Scotland, was walled up in Edinburgh Castle when he got news of the King's exploits in Carrick and the slaying of Percy's men. He called his council of war, and they decided to send Sir Ingram Bell, a sturdy knight, to Ayr with instructions to seek out Bruce and attack him with a great company of English soldiery. But when Ingram got there, he deemed it inexpedient to try to attack the King openly when all the advantage of mountain terrain was with him. So he sought to slay the King by treason, inquiring here and there for a suitable man to do it. Now there was a Carrick man of great strength and cunning, like most Carrick men, and he was trusted by the King, whose near kinsman he was. He had done some service to the King, he and his two sons, by warning him against approaching enemies, although they were unwilling to declare themselves openly for the Scottish cause. He had easy access to the royal presence, for all these reasons, and Ingram now bribed him to slay the Bruce. What the man's name was tradition has not preserved, but he was said to be one-eyed and the most powerful man in the Carrick lands.

Sir Ingram tested the man slyly, and being assured of his aptitude for the role of treacherous assassin, promised him forty pounds' worth of land for ever, for himself and his heirs, to murder the King. The man agreed to this bargain and went home to await his opportunity to perpetrate the crime. The King was in great danger, for he had an open nature, once he had decided a

43

man was trustworthy, and his free and fearless ways would have left him vulnerable to such treachery. But by the grace of God word of the villainous pact leaked out to the Scots and Bruce therefore was put on his guard. It is not recorded who gave the warning, but Bruce seemed always to be lucky in this way, otherwise his natural fearlessness would have betrayed him to an assassin's dagger on a number of occasions. It is said that even the women he solaced himself with in the days of his hardship and separation from the Queen kept him informed of all they could pick up of local gossip or hearsay, and so it may have been on this occasion. But anyway, he was forewarned and accordingly vigilant.

The traitor, casting in his mind for a suitable occasion for the planned murder, remembered that the King had a habit of rising early every morning and going to relieve nature in some private bush or such nearby, with never more than one man to keep watch for him, and usually alone. This was the assassin's main problem – to get him alone and at a disadvantage. A little reconnoitring soon disclosed the particular spot near the present camp, and next day the man and his sons lay in wait for the King.

At his usual time the King went out to this early morning privacy, but because of the warning he wore his sword round his neck. He had only a page boy with him, and the clump of bushes was on the other side of the hill, out of sight of his men. Now the assassins felt secure in their secrecy, fully believing that the King was unaware of their villainy, and, knowing his usual generosity of nature, they came up to meet him quite openly. But the King at once grabbed a bow from his page boy and fitted an arrow to it, and told the boy to stand away up the hill and watch. The traitors came on, the father bearing a sword, one son a sword and an axe, and the other a sword and a spear. Even if the King had not been told of their perfidy, he could scarcely have mistaken their purpose – but he himself would have been unarmed. Now he challenged them.

'Traitor,' he shouted, 'not another step forward or you die. You have sold me to the English. Stand where you are.'

'Sire, you mistake me,' said the traitor. 'Who has more right than I to come near you as a bodyguard, being your own kinsman?'

'Not a step further,' said the King, 'I command you on my royal authority.'

The traitors, however, full of ingratiating words, kept advancing, so the King swiftly drew the bow and let fly against the evil flatterer, and the father fell pierced to the brain through the eye. The first brother now leapt at the King and struck at him with his axe, but the Bruce had his sword out in a trice and dealt him such a deft and powerful backhanded blow as the axe swished past that the skull was split right into the brain-pan. Bruce had barely time to wrench his sword free when the third man came at him full force with his spear, his face contorted with grief and rage. The King dodged the thrust and struck off the head of the spear with his sword as it passed, then swung up his sword in recovery from the same stroke and came down full force on the back of the man's head, splitting open his skull and hurling him a blood-red heap on the ground.

The King, breathing a bit heavily from his exertions, wiped the gore from his sword-blade, and looked hard at the men on the ground. His page came running up to him, saying, 'God be praised that He has granted you the mighty strength to slay so quickly three proud felons.'

The Bruce looked up and sighed, saying, 'As God is my witness, I mourn the loss of three such valiant kinsmen. But they were full of treachery and that has been their undoing.'

Bruce Defends His Men at a Ford

SIR INGRAM BELL soon came to hear of the fate that had befallen the traitor he had sent against the King, and he was furious that his cunning plot had thus miscarried. He reported the matter to Sir Aymer de Valence, who was astonished that one man could achieve such a feat of arms in such circumstances.

'Truly', he said, 'here we see how fate always favours the brave. This deed is the proof. If he had not been so outstandingly brave he could not ever come out of it alive. Such prowess, I fear, will bring his struggle to a conclusion I have no desire to see.'

Bruce meantime was kept on the run in Carrick, his men so scattered that scarcely sixty of them remained with him. The Galloway people got to know this, and collected a posse of some 200 men to hunt him down, and they took a hound with them to help track him if he should give them the slip. They hoped to surprise him by night, and made straight for the place where they knew he was hiding. But Bruce always had scouts planted at every strategic approach, and was warned of their coming in ample time to slip away with his men in the gathering darkness.

Following a plan he had in mind, he led them down to a swampy place, crossed a running river in the middle of it, and settled his men about a couple of bow-shots from it. 'Lie and rest here a while', he said, 'and I will keep watch at the ford we have just crossed, and warn you if they come near it.'

He left Sir Gilbert Haye in charge of the men and took only two servants with him to the ford. There being no sign of the enemy, he reconnoitred a mile or two up and down the river and ascertained that there was no other place they might cross except this narrow ford, so he could not be outflanked. On his side of the river, too, the bank was very steep, with only a narrow defile up which men could come from the water, and that only in single file. He then sent his servants back to sleep with the others, that they too might get some rest: and when they protested that he would be left alone, he told them this was not so, as God would be with him.

After some time the King heard the baying of a hound, far off at first, but coming nearer and nearer. The night was very still and dark, and the King stood listening intently, undecided whether this was some innocent foraging

dog or something more sinister. Reluctant to rouse his men in some trivial cause, he decided to wait and see what happened. The moon rode out of the clouds and so brightened up the scene that he soon made out the whole posse pressing on towards the ford. The King now realised that if he went to warn the men, the enemy would mostly be over the ford before the men could stop them. He therefore made the bold decision to stand at the top of the defile and cut down each man as he struggled up from the ford. He was fully armed and proof against all but the unlucky arrow, and his courage and pride reinforced his military judgement that one man in such a place might indeed stop an army. Thus resolved, the King took up his position at the head of the defile and flexed himself to face 200 men alone.

The enemy saw the solitary figure standing on the far bank, his armour glinting in the moonlight, and thronged into the water to the attack. They had no doubt at all of the outcome and couldn't get at him fast enough. But the first man up the defile found himself struck to earth with the King's short stabbing-spear, held in his left hand. As the others tried to swarm up, the King also stabbed the horse of the man he had killed so that it lashed out with its hooves backward at the men, and fell blocking the path. Still they came on and the King hacked at them to such effect with his mighty sword-arm that soon another five lay dead in the pass. The others, for the first time doubting the success of their sheer numbers, drew back in wonder at the phenomenon above them. But their leader rallied them by reminding them of the shame of allowing one man thus to rout so many – they would never dare lift their heads again.

They rushed the pass again with shouts of 'On him, upon him, he cannot last out', pressing forward with such ardour that no ordinary man could possibly have stood against them. But the Bruce was no ordinary man, and he made such powerful defence of this position that nothing could stand against his strokes. In very little time he had slain so many that the pass was choked with the bodies of men and horses, so that the men behind had no chance of even reaching the bank. They were defeated and fell back.

Never have I heard before of such a feat of arms, and any man who had watched that mighty struggle in the weird moonlight would have acclaimed Bruce the greatest man of his time. It is doubtful whether even Tydeus, who once slew fifty men in a moonlight encounter, surpassed the deed: for though he slew more men than Bruce, he undid only a quarter as many.

By this time the din of battle at the ford had wakened the King's men, and when they hurried up, they found him sitting alone in the moonlight, his basnet by his side, wiping the sweat from his face and neck, and panting with exertion. He told them what had happened and how God had given him the victory over 200. And when they examined the pass, they found no less than fourteen men slain by his own hand, and several horses: and Bruce's men knelt and gave thanks to God for saving their lord whole, and for the awesome might of valour by which this one man had saved their own lives unaided.

Bruce and the Hound of Lorne

THE fame of King Robert's deeds of valour spread like a summer sunrise and men marvelled at his achievements. Valour is greatly to be prized, but it has two attendant extremes which have to be avoided – recklessness and cowardice. True valour steers a course between them, and indeed can scarcely exist without good sense. Now the King's valour was at all times the servant of his wisdom, and the great courage and skill of arms he demonstrated at the ford would have gone for nothing without the keen intelligence and good judgement that saw the possibilities of that particular defile at the ford. Bruce was a master in the use of terrain in warfare and never made a serious mistake in his whole career, and the fight at the ford is but one example of this ability of his to make terrain fight for him like an army.

After the ford incident the King and his men got to Carrick where he rested for a while, but his men were still scattered on all sides. The news of the ford drew them towards him, determined to share his fate whatever it should be, but times were still unpropitious. Douglas was on the run in Douglasdale, having still to hide like a hunted fox, but spying and biding his time for guerilla raids. He learned that the new governor of the castle would openly ride out with his company, so he gradually got together a troop of men big enough to challenge this Thirlwall and the garrison.

One night he laid an ambush at Sandilands with his men, and carried out this plot. About daybreak a few of the men slipped out and rounded up cattle that were grazing near the castle, and drove them towards the ambush. The castle guard gave the warning and Thirlwall at once armed his men and rode out in pursuit. He himself led, fully armed except for his head, which was uncovered. They chased the cattle well into the ambush, recklessly spread out

49

in disorder. Then the Douglas men leapt out, shouting their battle-cry. The garrison took fright, seeing the sudden apparition of a troop of determined Scots between them and the retreat to the castle and, being in such disorder instead of compactly knit round their leader, some panicked and fled, others rode singly into the fray and were easily cut down. Thirlwall himself was one of the latter, reckless and incompetent as a commander, throwing away his life and leaving his men to be cut down leaderless. Some managed to escape, but most were slain where they stood and fought. Douglas and his men immediately rode fast after the fleeing men, and while the first few of them got into the castle, the bulk were overtaken and slain without mercy. The frightened garrison quickly barred up the castle-gates and manned the walls, but Douglas contented himself with seizing everything that could be found outside the castle walls, and made their escape.

Douglas now got word that Sir Aymer de Valence was himself riding north with a great host of Englishmen and Scottish traitors, determined to finish off the Bruce. He therefore hurried to the King, who was at this time hiding in an inaccessible area in Cumnock, and told the King that Sir Aymer was coming to hunt him down like a wolf or a thief with bloodhound and horn. The King said simply, 'We shall see. It may yet be that for all his power he will not find it so easy to shift us out of this country.'

Now Sir Aymer joined forces with John of Lorne, that arch-traitor and enemy of Bruce and Scotland, who had in his possession a certain hound which men say once actually belonged to Bruce himself. How it came into Lorne's possession I know not, but the tradition is very strong on this point, and it is even said that Bruce had reared the beast with his own hands, and that it loved him, this adding to its eagerness to track him down, once it got scent of him. Lorne, of course, was motivated simply by vengeance for the murder of his uncle Comyn, and was Bruce's most bloodthirsty enemy. He had about 800 men with him at this time and these he joined to Sir Aymer's host against the Bruce and his handful of retainers, whom they now came to hunt down in Cumnock.

The King's scouts kept him well informed of every move the enemy made, and he retreated into the utmost fastness the terrain could afford him, with 300 men, including his brother and James Douglas. But when the King from the heights looked down at the host advancing in full battle array under Sir Aymer's pennon, he had no idea that he was not seeing the whole host. He did not know that John of Lorne had branched off and was creeping up on him from behind, under cover of the trees. Bruce was thus caught in a pincer-movement from the two armies, and was in great danger. Both armies were much larger than his own small force. But when he saw that his position was untenable, he took swift counsel, split his force into three parts, each

making its escape in a different direction. Thus he hoped to confuse his pursuers and throw them onto the wrong scent. But when John of Lorne came up to the abandoned position, the hound very quickly picked up the scent of its old master, and went baying excitedly after him.

Bruce quickly realised that they were on to him already, and again tried the tactic of splitting the group into three, each going off in different directions. But again the hound unerringly followed its master. The King could not understand what was happening, and was puzzled at the assurance with which they seemed to know him and his whereabouts. So this time he ordered all his men to scatter, each fending for himself, the King taking only his foster-brother with him. But the hound could not be fooled and un-erringly picked up the scent of Bruce from all others, with Lorne exultantly behind him. Then Lorne, sure he had isolated his man, bade five of his best and swiftest men run him down. In no time at all they were almost on top of the King. When Bruce saw there were only five of them he was minded to take them on, but considered that, if they were good fighters, he might waste so much time on them that the others would catch up. But after a quick word with his companion, he decided to fight, and turned determinedly to face them as they came noisily on. Three went straight for the King, while the other two rode at his kinsman. The first man went down to the King's mighty sword-arm with a cloven skull sheered right to the shoulder. The other two had never seen such a blow and started back amazed. The King took advantage of this to leap at the two who were fighting his kinsman and slew one with another mighty blow that took the head from his shoulders. Then he turned again to meet his own two opponents, smote the arm from the shoulder of the first, and the other two men were quickly slain. The King's foster brother gave Bruce all the credit for four of the slain, but Bruce gave his kinsman his full due, making light of his own part.

Drenched with sweat, exhausted, they plunged down through the wood with Lorne and the baying hound close at their heels, down to where a stream ran through the glen. The King was tiring badly and in desperate need of rest, but his kinsman urged him on. Arrived at the stream, the King remembered that a hound cannot pick up a trail in water, so they entered the stream and waded down it for about a bow-shot length before coming out on the other side and forging on.

Meanwhile Lorne paused briefly to lament the men slain by the King and his kinsman, then pressed on the faster to avenge them. He came very quickly to the bank of the stream, where the hound ran up to the very edge then stopped, baffled. It sniffed all round about but the trail led only to the river and stopped. Lorne realised that by the time they crossed the stream and picked up the scent again, either well up or well down the river, Bruce would be out of the forest and escaped. So with angry acceptance of what could not be mended, he gave up the chase and took his men back to join the main body of troops.

Thus the King escaped his pursuers. Another tale of this escape I have heard says that the King had with him an expert archer who never left his side, and that he, when they had become aware of the fact that it was a hound they were unable to shake off, hid himself nearby and as it came up slew it with a single arrow. But whichever tale is true, certain it is that the King made a lucky escape from the hound of Lorne.

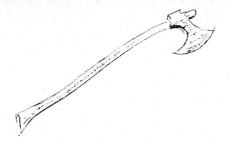

The Price of Sleep

WHILE John of Lorne told the marvelling Sir Aymer of Bruce's latest exploit, the King and his kinsman won out of the forest and on to a wide high moor. About half-way across it they saw three men loafing towards them. They carried swords and axes and one of them had a sheep bound up on his shoulders. They hailed the King as they came up, and he returned the greeting, asking them where they were going. They said they wanted to join up with Robert the Bruce, if they could find him.

'If that is indeed your wish,' said the King, whose clothing in no way distinguished him, 'come with me and I'll lead you to him.'

Now the men knew, as soon as he spoke and they had taken in his general bearing, that this man was himself clearly a king and could be no other than the Bruce. And they began to show signs of unease, and to put on a feigned friendliness. For these men were in fact enemies of the King and sought to come upon him secretly and treacherously slay him as soon as they got the chance. But the Bruce missed nothing and saw the enmity and subterfuge in their manner.

'Friends,' said he, 'until we get to know each other better I prefer that you precede us on the journey, and we will follow close behind.'

'There's no need to think any ill of us, sir,' said they.

'Nor do I,' said he, 'it's just that I want you to walk ahead till we get to know each other better.'

They saw that the King was not a man to argue with, and did as they were ordered.

In this manner they came to a big farmhouse just at sunset, and there the men slaughtered the sheep they had been carrying, and made a fire to roast the meat. They invited the King to join them and rest up while they cooked the mutton. Bruce readily agreed, being famished, as you can imagine. But

53

he saw to it that he and his companion kept to a fire at one end of the house, while the men built another to cook on at the other end. They didn't argue with him, knowing their man, but sent him half the sheep when it was cooked, and ate their own ravenously.

Now the King had been on the run for a long time during which he had eaten very little, and he now made up for lost time. And when at last he felt satisfied, he began to relax, and the great strain and weariness of the chase brought an irresistible urge to sleep. When he realised that he could not keep awake, he said to his kinsman, 'Can I trust you to keep watch for a bit

while I get some sleep?' And the foster-brother said he would keep awake as long as he could before wakening the King to take over.

Bruce therefore dozed off, but so keen was his training and sense of danger that he but slept as birds do, with one eye open, watching the three men. But his kinsman was in much worse case, and without realising it he sank into a heavy sleep, oblivious to the world.

The King was now in great danger, for in his own drowsy state he was likely to drop off into deeper sleep and so be slain – for the men were watching intently from the other end of the room. At last, assured that the King and his companion were both asleep, the men tip-toed towards him with axe and sword. Half-way up the hall the King suddenly jerked awake and saw them. In a trice, as by reflex action, he was on his nimble feet with drawn sword in his hand. He kicked his kinsman with one foot as he rose to meet the traitors, but the man was so sleepy that before he could get to his feet one of the traitors sent him to a sleep from which there is no awaking.

The King was then in a tighter corner than he had yet known, and but for the light armour under his disguise he would certainly have been slain. But, despite the cramped circumstances which gave him little room for footwork and manœuvre, he so fought that by God's grace and his own manly skill he slew all three of the traitors. The Bruce was sorely grieved at the death of his foster-brother, partly blaming himself and partly the assassins, and in this mood of anger and grief he made his way alone to the place of meeting arranged with his men when they had had to separate in the chase.

Bruce Acquires Two Men and Douglas Returns

WHEN Bruce arrived at the house where he and his men were to meet, it was very late at night, but he found the goodwife sitting up. She asked him brusquely who he was, where he came from, and where he was going.

'I am a homeless man forced to wander about the country,' said the King.

'All such men are welcome here for the sake of one particular homeless wanderer,' said the goodwife.

'And who might he be, madam,' said the King, 'who causes you to have such a good heart for the homeless wanderer?'

'That I am proud to tell you,' replied the goodwife. 'That one is our rightful King, Robert the Bruce, who is the true lord of all this land. He is now sore oppressed by his enemies and ours, but I know that before long I shall see him lord and King of the whole country and master of all his enemies.'

'And do you indeed love him so well, madam?' asked the King.

'Indeed I do, sir, as God is my witness,' she answered.

'Then lady, take a good look at the wanderer before you, for I am the man you speak of.'

The goodwife looked up at the noble, weather-beaten face above her, the great head and brow, the broad cheekbones and proud nose, the strong, lined mouth, and said falteringly, 'Are you telling me the very truth?'

'Indeed I am, lady,' Bruce replied.

'But your men, Sire, your men – where have they gone, that you should be left thus unattended?'

'Madam,' he replied, 'at this minute I don't have a single one of them.'

'That is something that cannot be allowed,' she cried, 'and shall not be. I have two bold sons, good men of their hands, and they shall become your men at once.'

She called her sons and they were glad to obey her wish, and the King received them as gladly into his fealty as his own men. The goodwife then set the table for him and set him down to eat. He was but half-way through the meal, however, when there was a great clatter of hooves and commotion about the house. The woman's sons at once leapt to the defence of their lord, but in a trice the door burst open and in stepped James Douglas. The King joyfully embraced him in comradely arms, and quickly invited in all the others who were with him, his own brother Sir Edward Bruce among them. Behind these leaders were a body of 150 stalwart men. It was a joyful reunion, and the King was asked about his escape. He told them the whole tale of the Hound of Lorne, the five men, the escape down the stream, the attempt of the three sheep-stealers to murder him in his sleep, and the death of his foster-brother.

Thus they spent the evening talking back and forth about their experiences. At last the King brought the talk back to the present and the future.

'We've had some very bad luck today, being scattered so suddenly by a turn of Fortune's wheel. Yet our enemies sleep safe in their beds to-night, secure in the belief that it will take three or four days to re-unite us all. Therefore if we knew where they are camping we might easily fall upon them and do great damage with only a handful of men, and escape without loss,' he said.

'Indeed,' said Douglas, 'and by good luck I happen to know where they are, for I chanced to come past their quarters on my way here. If we hurry we can do them more damage before dawn than they have done to us all day, for they lie scattered about the place.'

They were all of one mind about this, and set out at once, coming upon the sleeping camp just as the first light began to appear. They had found out that a company had broken away from the main body of troops and quartered in a village about a mile or so from the camp – about 2000, it is said. The King decided to attack this company and, having drawn up his force above the village, they charged at once. The most appalling uproar ensued, as the sleeping village was ransacked by sword and spear. Naked men stumbled out, dragging their arms behind them, or simply fled in panic all over the place. Bruce and his men slew grimly without mercy and with the utmost speed, and took such cruel revenge of their oppressors that it is said two-thirds of the whole company were slain, the rest escaping to the main body. And when the main army saw them come hollering and clamouring half-naked among them, some sorely wounded among them, the whole army rose in fright and prepared for action. But the King and his men were already fast retiring to the hills.

Once again Sir Aymer marvelled at the man he was set against, and said, 'This clearly shows how a noble heart is hard to subdue by force, whatever the circumstances. Given freedom, a valiant heart can so surmount all difficulties that no fear can dismay it, as this raid upon us demonstrates. We judged Robert the Bruce to be so dismayed by the day's setbacks that he would have no spirit left for such a fight. But his heart is unconquerable in its valour.' Thus spoke Sir Aymer – but being no such man himself, he gave up the pursuit of Bruce as sheer folly, and retired to the castle of Carlisle until such time as he might be able to surprise Bruce with a great force and beat him in pitched battle.

King Bruce and the Three Archers

BRUCE now stayed in his own Carrick lands for a time with all his men, with some of whom he would sometimes go hunting. But one day he was out alone with his two hounds, having got separated from his men. He sat down to rest at the edge of a wood, armed only with his sword, which he always carried. He had not been sitting long when he saw three men with bows in their hands hurrying towards him. A swift appraisal of their demeanour assured him that they were no friends of his, and he quickly released his hounds from their leash. Now these men were of the Comyn faction, deadly foes of the King, and sought only to be avenged on him for the death of Comyn. They had been lurking about for days, waiting for their chance, and now they thought it had come. Great was the King's danger, never his need of his strength and intelligence greater, and only the grace of God could make these of any use. For he had no armour on against arrows, and no bow of his own with him. They could strike him down from a distance and make their own escape unmolested.

As they came towards him, bending their bows to the string, the Bruce, acutely aware of his peril, shouted to them, 'You should be ashamed of yourselves, three to one, and fit only to shoot from a distance. You call yourselves men? If you've any spunk in you at all, come and try me with your swords – if you conquer me manfully, your fame will be great among men: but if you shoot me like an animal, men will despise you.'

The men stopped, and one of them said, 'By the Lord, no man shall say that I feared a Bruce or needed arrows to slay him.' And they threw down their bows and came on.

The King was greatly relieved by this and met them boldly with drawn sword. They were no match for his art, and the first of them was stretched dead on the grass with the first stroke from the King. The other two were upon him fast, but one of the King's hounds leapt at one of them and knocked him down with a fierce spring at the throat. The King at once severed his spine with a sword-thrust, and the third man turned and ran. But the King's hound was after him in a flash and pulled him down, while Bruce ran up and slew him.

Some of the King's men now appeared out of the wood, having been just in time to see the end of the action, and they came hastily up and inquired after him and what had happened. The King explained to them, and they expressed their admiration of his skill in getting out of so tight a situation unscathed, and having killed his three assailants. But the King demurred, saying he had only killed one man, really, while God and the hound had slain the other two. 'Indeed,' said he, 'they were disarmed by their own treason, for they were proper men of their hands, all three.' Then he sounded his horn, got all his men together, and returned home.

The Battle of Glentrool Forest

BRUCE lay at Glentrool for some time after this, taking pleasure and recreation in hunting the deer, which were then in season, to feed his men. But meantime the patient Sir Aymer de Valence was waiting at Carlisle for his chance to take Bruce, and his spies reported every move the King made. And when he heard of the Glentrool pastimes, he thought he saw his chance to fall on Bruce suddenly with an army while he was out hunting. He could leave Carlisle and make a forced march through the night, keeping cover by day, and soon be in a position to ambush the King. So he got together a large army of tried and renowned soldiers, both English and Scots, and in the manner described soon arrived at Glentrool. They occupied the nearby forest without Bruce being aware of their coming.

The Scots were now in great danger, for Sir Aymer's men were six to one against them.

I have been told that when Sir Aymer stopped in the woods within a mile of the Bruce, he called a council about what action to take. He pointed out that Bruce's encampment was impregnable owing to the high terrain and narrow approaches – only infantry could come at it, and they would be defeated if the Scots were warned, as inevitably they would be, of their coming. So he counselled that a woman be sent to spy on Bruce, poorly dressed, begging charity, and secretly noting all the camp arrangements, and report back the details. Then it might be possible for them to slink up quietly by night and take the Scots by surprise.

This plan was approved, and a woman was sent to the tents where the King, fearing no sudden attack, went happily about among his men, unarmed. He quickly perceived the woman, and his suspicions were at once aroused. So he had her seized at once and questioned, and she, fearing for her own life, told them the whole plan, and how Sir Aymer with Clifford and other English chivalry were lying there in the forest.

Bruce at once armed all his men, some 300 in all as I have heard, and the King raised his banner for all to see, and went among his men raising their morale and setting them in order, briefing them on their duties. And they waited thus for the coming of the English. They had not long to wait, for the English, expecting to meet the woman close by, came hurrying through the woods on foot, well armed, spears in hand. When they were near enough, the Bruce took a bow and arrow from one of his archers and loosed it at the foremost enemy, striking him full on the throat, splitting windpipe and gizzard so that he fell choking to the ground. Then the war-cries tore the air, and the tumult of battle was begun. The King seized his banner from his standard-bearer and charged down himself, crying, 'Upon them, upon them, they are all conquered!' He was first in the fight and mightily that great sword-arm rose and fell upon their heads. His men were inspired by his hardihood and courage and laid on, even the most timid of them, and so furiously they fought that soon all the vanguard of the enemy was cut to pieces. At sight of this, those who came behind began to fall back, and soon they were in full flight. The Bruce slew few of them, for their legs fought better than their arms. Thus were 1500 men or so beaten by a handful because their plan of surprise was outwitted by the King, and their poor morale faced with the fury of the Scots defence undid them disgracefully, and they shamed themselves forever. This shame was made worse by the recriminations that followed, for Clifford and Vaux came to blows over it. Sir Aymer calmed them, with difficulty, and knowing that nothing further could be done with such a demoralised pack of troops, he wisely withdrew to Carlisle with more shame than he had left behind him there.

The Battle of Loudoun Hill

AFTER this event Bruce brought his men out of the hill country and into the plains, for he now began to feel more confidence in their ability to strike back against great odds, and he wanted to finish the job he had begun. He first subdued Kyle and brought most of the men there into the King's peace, then did the same with the Cunningham country.

Sir Aymer moved to Bothwell, and was very cut-up by his recent reverses and Bruce's progress, and was determined to be avenged. So he sent Sir Philip Mowbray with, I have been told, about a thousand men, into Kyle to make war on the King. But Douglas had his spies everywhere and soon knew of their intentions and even the route they would come by, down Makyrnock's Way. So he took sixty men secretly of his own company and lay in ambush at the Edryford, on Makyrnock's Way, a spot between two deep bogs where no horse could pass, and with a wall of cliff at one side, at the foot of which Douglas lay with his men, using the cliff to protect their backs. They could see the enemy afar off, but could not be seen themselves.

They lay in ambush all night, and when the sun was well up in the morning, they saw the English vanguard advancing with full bannered array, with their infantry marching behind. As soon as the vanguard had thinned out and begun to pick its way across the narrow ford between the two bogs, Douglas and his men rushed out upon them shouting their war-cry. They let fly with bow and arrow, causing great havoc so that those behind began to withdraw, and sword and spear finished off the foremost. Some were drowned in the bog trying to escape, for wherever they turned there was no way out of the trap. Mowbray himself, who was in the very van of the fight, got away by

sheer valour. He charged straight into the Douglas ranks and broke a way
through, and a man who seized his scabbard and hung on as he passed was
dragged along at his horse's side till the sword-belt broke and the man was
left on the ground with his trophy. Once clear, Mowbray looked back to see
whether anything might be done for his men, but seeing them fleeing on all
sides and the impossibility of charging back through the Douglas men, he
gave discretion its head and rode home via Kilmarnock and Ardrossan, a long
way round. He was well received by the large English garrison at the castle,
despite the defeat, for they had great respect for his own manner of escape
and long solitary ride home.

Douglas made a great killing at Edryford, and Sir Aymer once again had
salt rubbed in his wounds as his routed men slunk back to Bothwell with the

news. But the Bruce was rejoiced in heart by this daring exploit of his young follower, and all his men were greatly cheered by the news.

The King now occupied Galston, which is opposite Loudoun, and took the people of that part into his peace. Sir Aymer was growing more and more restive and found it intolerably galling that Bruce should now actually rule part of the country, no longer being hunted from one hidy-hole to another, but governing the people. So he sent word to Bruce challenging him to an open battle on the tenth of May under Loudoun Hill, saying that Bruce's renown would be greater if he could win such a battle than by his un-chivalrous guerilla warfare. It was the same kind of argument Bruce himself had used against the three archers, but whatever the wisdom of it, the King was not a man lightly to take a slight to his honour. He thought seriously about the challenge, then gave this answer to the messenger: 'Tell your lord that if he dares to march an army against me I shall indeed meet him, if God spares me till then, on that day.'

The messenger rode quickly to Sir Aymer and told him Bruce's reply. Sir Aymer rejoiced, for he was certain that in open battle his sheer superiority of numbers and arms against the Scots must end in irrecoverable defeat for the King. And indeed there was reason in this.

What Sir Aymer was unable to make allowance for was the fact that his opponent was a soldier of genius, and that he could make the very ground he fought on count for thousands of men – he had as large an army in the terrain itself as ever he mounted in the field. And this genius Bruce now brought into play. He studied carefully the ground around Loudoun Hill, how the highway along which Sir Aymer must ride lay through a flat grassy terrain, but that on either side of the field, only a bowshot from the road, was a great bog, wide and deep. Bruce let his imagination run over the probable features of the forthcoming battle and decided that the field was too wide for a stand against cavalry. But it was the best ground available, and he set about im-proving it to his own advantage. He had three ditches cut across from each of the two bogs to the road, a bowshot apart from each other, and he made them so deep and sheer that men could not pass them without great trouble and loss of time. But close to the road he left passes broad enough to let about 500 through at a time. He thus created a sort of bottle-neck which prevented the whole mass of the English army coming on him together, and reduced it to a mere splash of cavalry at a time. The terrain was such that he knew he could not be attacked from the rear, and the bogs protected his flanks. He then re-surveyed the battle-field and was satisfied that he had chosen the best avail-able ground and properly prepared it as a powerful ally of his defence policy.

To complete this plan, he dug three fighting trenches for his men, putting some in the first, some in the second, and some in the third, while he and his

mounted troops were arrayed behind. The approaching English army therefore would be forced to thin out because of the three ditches, and when the
first decanting of them (for it was indeed like decanting a measure of wine)
got through, it would be held by the first trench: when it got past that, it
would be held by the second trench: then past that by the third: and those
Englishmen who managed to get through this obstacle race would then be
so few that Bruce and his cavalry would cut them in pieces as soon as they
arrived.

He then assembled his men and saw to their training and instruction in the
nature of the battle and his plan of campaign. He had in all about 600 men
and various camp followers and small folk, and with these he went on the
eve of the battle to the village of Little Loudoun and waited there to watch
for the coming of the English.

Sir Aymer, on his side, gathered a great force, about 3000 strong, well
armed and accoutred, and advanced chivalrously to the appointed tryst. On
the day of the battle, they made their way swiftly along the road to Loudoun
Hill, arriving nearby when the sun was already shining brightly in the sky,
flashing on the shields and armour of his splendid squadrons.

Bruce was up early and watching for their coming, two squadrons of them
in close order, one behind the other. Their helmets shone like fire in the sunlight, and what with the light reflected from these and from shields, spears,
pennons, and the like, the whole field was lit up. The banners were of bright
embroidery, the horses caparisoned with many colours, and the whole shining
splendour glittered like a regiment of angels.

'Gentlemen,' said the King, 'you now see there the powerful fellows who
would slay us all if they could, marching upon us with that intention.
Therefore, knowing their wickedness, let us go forward together and confront
them so boldly and resolutely that the hardiest man among them will turn
chicken-hearted. For if we meet the vanguard with the utmost ferocity and
utterly savage it, you will see the morale of the others flag at once. Pay no
attention to the fact that, in the mass, they outnumber us, for I have seen to it,
by my ditches, that in the actual fighting they will be in fact fewer at a time
than we are. Therefore, let each man stand forth powerfully for Scotland and
his own honour. Think what joy awaits us if, as I am confident will happen,
we gain the victory over our enemies. There will be no more need to fear
any man born of woman in this land of ours!'

And those who stood around the King said, 'Sire, be assured that under
God we will so conduct ourselves and discharge our duties that no blame can
be put upon us ever.'

'Then forward to the trenches,' said the King, 'and may the Lord preserve
us and guide us in the ways of righteousness for His own sake. Advance!'

At that the main body sped towards the first ditch, intending to meet the first charge head on at the narrows, then if need be, fall back upon the trenches behind them. The King himself, instead of directing from behind, confidently expected to win at the first encounter and rode to the very front with his men. The psychological effect of this on both sides was worth the risk, for it fired the Scots and dismayed the English. Only the camp-followers and small folk of no fighting importance were left behind on the hill.

Sir Aymer saw the King thus riding boldly forward down the hill to the plain, confident of success even in pitched battle, and to counteract this he

MOWBRAY   Sable, a lion Rampant Argent.

fired his men with promises of rewards and tales of their fame and glory if any of them could overcome the Bruce and gain victory over him. Then, as the Bruce and his men were now down on the plain, he sounded the charge, and the vanguard of his cavalry set spur to horse at the blast of the trumpets and charged forward close-packed behind their broad shields. With heads lowered on their horses' necks and spears couched at the level, they aimed straight for the King. Bruce and his men met their charge with such skill and hardihood that the best of the English van were unhorsed at once. Such a din of cracking and splintering of spears rose among the shouts and cries of men sorely wounded as struck dread to the hearts of hearers. Hard was the combat there on foot as sword fell upon sword, shield clashed on shield, and stout men hacked and hewed at each other's heads and limbs.

Ah, Almighty God! see how the King's majesty bears him so hardily against foes, his brother beside him, inspiring their men with mighty deeds of valour! See how Douglas lays on, but lately a boy, man now in his grimness of onslaught, an inspiration to all beside him, avid of honour and knightly renown! See how the King's men stab with spear mercilessly rider and steed, both, till the blood pours red from wide wounds! Down go stricken horses, lashing out around them, knocking down men in their death-throes, laying them open to death-wounds.

Seeing the foe thus reeling and stricken, hard the King pressed keenly upon them, raining such terrible blows, like hammer on anvil, that many's the man fell never to rise again. Already the first ground behind the first ditch was littered with the slain, horses and men, for the Scots and English were equal in number there. Within a few minutes more than a hundred lay stretched on the greensward, and the English left standing were weak from the sight and the ferocity of the battle. They began to fall back, and when those in the rear saw their vanguard thus vanquished, they fled without further prompting. Sir Aymer stormed and raged at his troops in his vexation, but nothing could turn them back to that flailing massacre. And when he saw there was no help for it and all his trouble had gone for nothing, with an aching heart he turned his own horse's head and left the field. But Bruce pressed on them mercilessly and many more were slain and captured in the rout.

The English soldiery did not stop till they reached Bothwell, where Sir Aymer grieved sorely over his latest humiliating defeat. It was a mortal wound to his honour, and when he had recovered sufficiently from the shame, he rode straight to King Edward in England and in great anguish of spirit humbly resigned his command. So badly he took this defeat in pitched battle to heart, the defeat of a proud English army by a rabble of Scots guerillas in open battle, that he was never again seen in Scotland until he came, under King Edward himself, to do battle at Bannockburn, many years later. He was a knight of great renown and true valour, but no match for the good King Robert.

Bruce waited in the field till he had gathered together all his men again and marched with their prisoners back to their camp, joyfully praising God for His great benefaction to them that day. O to have seen our folk at last, after long hardship and intolerable oppression, merry and glad, relishing the fruits of victory on starved palates. And their lord, so amiable and jaunty, happy and full of fun, this mighty warrior so strong, prudent and wise in battle – good cause had they all to rejoice. And many men of the neighbourhood came and did homage to so successful a King.

James Douglas
in the Border Country

KING ROBERT now felt more and more certain of his powers, and that he might now march against his enemies in the north-east. He had one friend there in Sir Alexander Fraser and his family, for they were relatives of the King. But he had many enemies such as Sir John Comyn, Sir John Mowbray, and many others. It was against these that the King decided to try his strength, and he marched north with his men and such stalwart companions as his brother and Sir Gilbert Haye, Sir Robert Boyd, and the Earl of Lennox.

James Douglas was not among them. It had been agreed that he and his own men might stay and try to recover the Douglas lands in the south-west. It was a hard and dangerous task for a young man, but Douglas worked so bravely and well that he very soon brought into the King's peace the whole of Selkirk Forest, Douglasdale and Jedburgh. His deeds have not found their poet yet, and if one such ever appeared, he would have material enough to sing about. I have been told that Douglas won fifty-seven victories and suffered thirteen defeats in his time. He was a man of restless energy, never idle long, always seeking work for his hands. It is no wonder that he was loved and admired by the people.

One of his first exploits, when the King had left for the north-east, was to lay a secret plot to take his own castle in Douglasdale from the enemy. He made a very skilful and hidden ambush there, in the following manner. He got fourteen or so of his men to take sacks filled with grass straddled across their horses' backs and come down the path leading to Lanark, as if they were going to the fair. James and the rest were hidden in bushes at the side of the

road near the castle. As the laden horses passed by the ambush they were clearly visible to the castle, and the garrison looked greedily upon them. The captain, a certain Sir John Webton, a young harum-scarum wencher of a man, but fierce and strong in battle, immediately decided to grab the bait. He sent his men, fully armed, to seize the horses and their valuable loads, for the castle was always in need of victualling. All unsuspecting, forth they rode in no proper order, not expecting any difficulty in their robbery. They passed by the ambush in their pursuit of the prey, so that Douglas and his men were now between them and the castle. As soon as they came up with the loaded horses, the Douglas men in charge of the beasts threw off their peasant disguise from their well-armed bodies and seized the reins of the castle garrison horses. Before the castle men could recover from the shock, Douglas and his men sallied out from the ambush and hurled themselves into the fray. The castle men were hopelessly trapped and cut down without mercy as they fled hither and thither trying to escape. Sir John Webton himself was among the slain, and on his person was found a love-letter from a lady he was wooing in the courtly love manner. The lady had written to say that if he could keep the dangerous castle of Douglas for one year, governing it well in all ways, and remained chaste, at the end of it he might indeed receive her favours, and be allowed to make love to her.

Douglas wasted no time on reading love-letters, however, and rode at once straight to the castle, and so hammered it that he was soon inside it. I am not quite sure how this was achieved, whether by force or stratagem, but it seems that he very quickly captured all the remaining men in it, including the constable, and not only spared their lives but sent each one, men and boys, back to England with a present of money. Then, as he could not at this stage actually occupy his own castle or leave any of his men in it, he battered down the walls and destroyed the living quarters inside them. Then he and his men took to the forest again, and the many more adventures that befell them. The poet who could do justice to the exploits of Douglas would win himself great and enduring fame.

Perth Falls to the King

WE LEAVE the good James of Douglas there in the forest fighting manfully
for his heritage, and follow the noble King, who met up with the Frasers at
the Mounth. Right glad was the King at that meeting, and the kinsmen
welcomed each other. They told Bruce about the doings of the Comyn
faction under John Comyn, Earl of Buchan, and of their hatred of the King.

'There is nothing they would like better, Sire', said Alexander Fraser,
'than to avenge on you the murder of Sir John Comyn at Dumfries.'

'May the Lord forgive me that deed,' said the King, 'but truly I had great
cause to slay him. Since they feel they must make war on me and the kingdom because of Comyn, however, I must fight back against them, and let
God decide the issue.'

The King then hurried to Inverury, where he was prostrated by a dangerous
illness which so afflicted him that he could neither eat nor drink. His men
could not get proper medicine for him in these parts, and he soon became so
weak that he could neither walk nor ride. His men were deeply distressed, as
you can well believe, for there was no man among them who would not have
rather seen his own brother dead at his feet than the King so stricken, for they
all depended on him for their own good spirits; he was a great inspiration
to them. Sir Edward Bruce, the King's brother, did his best to keep up their
morale and cheer and strengthen them with his own superb courage. But
when the lords saw that the King got worse instead of better, they decided

that it would be wise to move him to a better place in the hills, where they would have a better chance of defending themselves against attack. So they sought out some fastness in the mountains till the King should recover from his illness.

Leadership is very important to most men, for there are few who will fight or work as well in a difficult pass alone as they will under a good leader, a man of daring, and trust in the will of God. Given a leader such as Bruce, a man of altogether exceptional qualities, his men take such inspiration from his manhood and bravery that each one becomes worth three of those who have no such inspiring leader. And on the other hand, a cowardly leader can so undermine his men that they become less even than they would be without him. For if the leader is no better than a corpse or a coward, will not his men be already defeated in their hearts? Ay, indeed they will, unless their hearts are sustained by valour of their own. And even then there will be some, however noble they may be, who will flee when they see their leader do so, for it is natural for men to shun death. Therefore you see how important is a courageous leader, for a cowardly one will infect his men with his own disease, whereas a truly noble one will inspire men to achieve the impossible.

Such a leader was King Robert. By his exceptional manhood he was such an inspiration to his men that none knew what fear was. But they had no wish to fight while he was lying ill, so they carried him in a litter to Sliach, a mountain fastness in the hills near Garioch, about sixteen miles above Inverury, determined to stay there until he got better.

The Earl of Buchan, however, heard of the plight of the King and where they had taken him, and he at once assembled his men, and joined forces with Mowbray and others to attack the stricken King at Sliach. They marched in full force against him, the time of the year Martinmas, and snow covered the whole country. The King's men were warned of their coming and prepared to defend their stronghold to the death, knowing the enemy two to one against them.

Buchan's men marched with great pomp and much sounding of trumpets and flaunting of their power. But the King's men stood firm, refusing to descend and fight, but ready to defend if attacked from below. Seeing this, the Earl sent his archers against them, but the King's archers gave such spirited reply that the Earl's retreated, and that skirmish was over. For three days the archers exchanged fire in this manner, but each time the Earl's were driven back. But despite this, the Earl's forces continued to grow, as more and more people came to join them, and the food problem grew acute. The King's men therefore decided to move on to a place where supplies would be easier come by. So they laid the King in a litter again and sallied forth under the full gaze of their enemies, grim men fully armed packed tightly round the King, and making no great hurry in case they caused him distress or pain. And at sight of them the Earl's men lost heart, or perhaps they felt some shame for their own position, and they made no attempt to attack but went home to Buchan. Sir Edward Bruce led his band to Strathbogie and stayed there till the King began to mend: and when he was able to walk about again, they returned to Inverury, wishing to winter in the plains where supplies would not fail.

There the Earl of Buchan decided to attack them, and gathered his scattered army together again and marched pompously to Old Meldrum. There they camped on the day before Christmas Eve 1307, about a thousand men in all. Sir David Brechin rode out the day before Christmas to reconnoitre in Inverury and came so suddenly on a party of King's men that he slew some and routed the others. The latter fled to the King, at the far end of the town, and told him the news. King Robert, though not yet fit to ride, at once called for his horse and ordered his men to prepare for battle. And he struggled to his feet.

'But Sire,' some of his men remonstrated, 'surely you cannot think of fighting and you not yet properly recovered from your illness!'

'Indeed I shall,' said the King, 'for their insolence has made me well again – no medicine could have revived me as this has done. As God is my witness I will either take them or they me!'

And when his men heard the vibrant ring again in his voice, they rejoiced and prepared enthusiastically for battle. The King had about 700 men in his army at this time, and with them they set out on the heels of Brechin for Old Meldrum, where the Earl of Buchan lay with his main host. The scouts saw them coming, banners waving in the breeze, and gave the alarm. Hurriedly the Earl mustered his men and prepared for battle. They made a fine show as they drew up their ranks, but part of this included the small folk whom they ranked up behind them, which made them look more numerous than they in fact were in terms of fighting men.

Bruce came on in great strength of arms, and the Earl's men made a great show of standing their ground till near the point of clash. But when they saw the grim figure of the noble King in full armour riding ferociously down upon them, they faltered and began to back away from the onslaught. And when Bruce saw this lack of morale, he pressed on all the harder. It was as if some invisible influence preceded the King, driving back the enemy until, without so much as breaking a lance, they turned and fled in confusion. When the small folk thus saw their Lords and masters fleeing, they too fled, adding to the rout.

Rarely has so brave a show come to such an ignominious end. The King's

men sped on after these cowards and slew or captured as many as they could, but most of them escaped, the men best horsed getting best away. The Earl fled to England, Mowbray with him, and sought refuge with King Edward there. But little good it did them, for these would-be challengers of the King of Scots died shortly in exile. Sir David Brechin fled to his own castle of Brechin and shut himself up in it with all the provender and arms he could lay hands on. But the Earl of Atholl's son David, who was in Kildrummy,

F

soon came to besiege him there, and Sir David Brechin, having no more heart to oppose his noble King, surrendered on good conditions and did homage to his lord.

Bruce was delighted with his victory and caused his men to burn the whole of Buchan from one end to the other, sparing none. He so ravaged that stubborn region that even now, seventy years later, men still lament the Ravage of Buchan. The King then took the whole of the north into his peace, and it humbly accepted his sovereignty so that north of the Mounth there was not a man out against him, and his rule increased throughout the land. He went then to Angus, planning soon to set free the whole country north of the Scottish Sea (the Firth of Forth).

At this time Forfar Castle was still garrisoned by the English, but one Philip, the forester of Platane, and some friends of his took ladders, climbed the stone wall and, thanks to a neglectful watch, took the whole garrison by surprise. Every man of them was put to the sword, and Philip yielded the castle to the King, who rewarded him handsomely for his enterprise. Then the King had the walls broken down and the well of the castle filled in.

Once Forfar had thus been reduced, the King, wise as he was active and brave, marched the whole army to Perth and besieged the town. It was no easy task to take it, for the walls were built high of solid stone with great high towers, and as long as there was enough provender inside it, the town could not be taken. Moffat and Oliphant lived in it at this time, together with the Earl of Strathearn (whose son had joined the Bruce), holding it for the English. There was a great deal of skirmishing went on here, dour and merciless in-fighting, and men were slain on both sides. The good King, perceptive in everything he did, satisfied himself that the town could not be taken by force of arms, and decided to try guile. He studied the moat carefully and at last found a place where a man might wade it, the water no higher than shoulder-level. The siege had gone on for about six weeks, and the King, briefing his men on his impending stratagem, had them pack up, and they all marched away as if lifting the siege. The people on the town walls mocked him as he passed, jeering and laughing at his supposed defeat. The King rode silently on, as if indeed abandoning the place. But he had ladders made secretly, enough for his purpose, and about eight days later he and his army slunk back to the town by dead of night. Then a party took the ladders and went swiftly on foot towards the walls.

The townsfolk had been so easily fooled by the retreat that they slept sound, expecting no danger, and their sentinels were nodding at their posts. Bruce listened carefully and, hearing no sound, took a ladder, and himself led his men through the icy moat, feeling his way with his spear. The King, who was an athletic man of above medium height, was up to his throat in water.

He was immediately followed by a valiant French knight who marvelled at the King's hardihood compared with the luxury-loving French nobles he knew best. The rest of Bruce's men followed, and they all put their ladders in place against the wall: then, at a signal from the King, they swarmed up together. I have been told that so active was the King that only one man beat him to the top, despite his armour. Bruce waited on the top till the whole force was up, and just as the last man made it, a cry of alarm went up from the garrison. But by now it was too late, for the King and his men were over. Some men were sent at once to open the gates and let in the main body of the army, and soon the whole town was in confusion as Bruce's men ran through it, taking easy possession of the sleeping burgh. By dawn, the whole place was safely under the King's command. Both wardens were captured, among others, and the Earl of Strathearn was taken captive by his own son: on account of which the King pardoned the Earl and restored his lands to him, for sake of his noble son. Others of the King's men ran through the town and seized great supplies of armour, merchandise, gear of all sorts, and many who had been poor as church mice before now found themselves rich and mighty with spoil. But very few died in that encounter, for the King had ordered that no more blood was to be shed than was absolutely necessary, for these towns-folk were Scots, not English.

Thus was Perth taken, and the King then caused the towers and walls to be destroyed, so that the enemy could never again use them against him without great trouble. The prisoners were sent into safe keeping and the whole countryside taken into the King's peace. The whole of Scotland north of the Scottish Sea was now ruled by Bruce, except the Lorne country of Argyll, which still relentlessly held out against the King: of which I will speak again later.

Sir Edward Bruce now set out with a large company for Galloway, determined to wrest that area from the English if he could. This Sir Edward was a noble knight and a great man of his hands. He was a large, jovial man of irrepressible courage and high spirits, but inclined to be a bit reckless. He feared nothing on two legs or four, and great was his renown among his peers, so that many a romance might be made of his doings. I can only relate a very small part of them here.

Sir Edward Bruce in Galloway

Sir Edward Bruce and his men reached Galloway in good time, and soon brought the country under his power. Sir Ingram Umphraville, a knight renowned for exceptional valour, lived in Galloway at this time, and he and Aymer de St. John governed the area between them. When they heard that Sir Edward was harrying the countryside and bringing it into his overlord-ship, they hurriedly mustered an army of some 1200 men, as I have heard. They greatly outnumbered Sir Edward's men, but when the two armies met up by the River Cree, Sir Edward immediately charged the enemy and so hammered them that he put the whole lot to flight and slew above 200 of them. Sir Ingram, who always had a red bonnet carried on a spear in front of him to signify his exalted chivalrous rank, escaped with Sir Aymer to Butel Castle, leaving the best of their men lying dead on the soil. Sir Edward was angry to have missed his prey, for they would have been worth a rich ran-som, so he carried off all the cattle he could lay hands on – a great number. The garrison of Butel looked on helplessly as their beasts were rustled and driven off.

The whole of Galloway was staggered by this astonishing feat of arms, and Sir Edward was much feared in the area. A number of men came and did homage to him, and were received into the King's peace. But Sir Aymer rode into England and there mustered a huge army to help him avenge the shame of his defeat by the noble Sir Edward. With a force of full 1500 men and more, all of them knights of renown, he set out to surprise Sir Edward if he could. And now I report a truly great feat of arms. The first thing that Sir Edward knew of Sir Aymer's advance was when a cry went up one early morning that the English were coming. He at once armed himself and was quickly in the saddle. He had no more than fifty men with him, all well armed and mounted, and he got his small folk to withdraw to a narrow defile nearby. With only these fifty men Sir Edward rode out, and what I am about to tell you was told to me personally by one of them, Sir Alan Cathcart, a knight of the utmost valour, courtesy and reputation, as I can vouch.

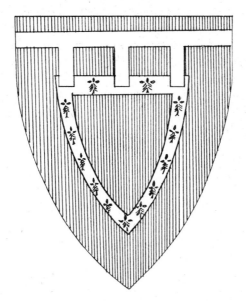

UMPHRAVILLE   Gules, an Orle Ermine, a label of 3 points Argent.

It happened that there was a great deal of mist about that morning, and men could not see a bow-shot because of it. By sheer good luck the little war-party stumbled on the trail their enemies had just left behind them, and Sir Edward, in his impulsive way, immediately rode after them. Just before noon the mist suddenly cleared away and the Scots saw the English army only a bow-shot in front of them. With a great shout Sir Edward charged at once, his men behind him, having no choice but flight or attack – and to flee would have ended in their massacre. But it is doubtful whether Sir Edward was motivated by anything but his own headlong daring.

The English were taken completely by surprise, and hadn't time to assess the actual number of the Scots who came riding down on them with such assurance as suggested a large army behind them. The Scots at once laid about them with such vigour that soon many a knight was stretched on the ground. Sir Aymer's men were in consternation as a result of this ferocious onslaught, and assumed that there must be a very large number of Scots coming up behind. Sir Edward's men, having cut right through the ranks of the English, rallied and charged back again, and again a great number of the enemy were borne down. This so demoralised the English that they began to scatter and flee, and at sight of this, Sir Edward rallied his men and charged once again a third time. This resulted in the total rout of the enemy, chased by Sir Edward and his men, slaying some and taking many prisoners. Sir Aymer himself escaped, but his army was wholly scattered and defeated.

From this it may be seen how a bold deed, done on the spur of the moment but with decision and determination and executed accordingly, may snatch victory from the jaws of certain defeat. But there can be few cases on record of fifty men overcoming 1500.

Sir Edward stayed in Galloway and in time brought the whole area into the King's peace, taking thirteen castles in a year. He lacked only the wisdom and prudence of his brother to make him his equal.

Douglas in Ettrick Forest

DURING all these events James Douglas was wandering in Ettrick Forest, harrying the enemy with guerilla warfare, never letting them rest, stemming their attacks on him and by sheer hardiness and daring stratagems managing to hold his own against great odds.

Now it happened that one night he was on his way to spend the night in a house on Lyne Water in Peeblesshire, and as he neared the place he heard voices coming from the house. He and his men halted and, creeping close, heard every word that was spoken within. Clearly strangers had taken over the place for the night, and he gradually learned who they were – some very important Scotsmen opposed to the King. Among them were Alexander Stewart, Lord of Bonkyl, that great ancestor of many Scottish earls of renown and of King James VI, Thomas Randolph, the King's nephew, and Adam Gordon. They were still enemies of the King and had come to the Forest, Douglas learned, in order to help hunt him out by means of their greater forces and high valour. But they had reckoned without their host, for Douglas now quietly surrounded the house and gave the signal for attack. The nobles within seized their weapons and rushed out. They had no chance, however, and Douglas wounded and captured Stewart, captured Randolph, and chased Gordon for his life.

It was a strange night that followed, for captor and captives, despite the circumstances, were men of a mould and were right glad to see each other. The Stewart was a cousin of Douglas's, Randolph a nephew of the King, and whatever motives held them to King Edward, blood is thicker than water, and there was great swopping of stories. Next day, Douglas mounted his prisoners and rode to meet the King at once and deliver them up.

Bruce was delighted at this coming, and with his important captives, and greatly he thanked the good Douglas for it.

'You have long been a faithless traitor to me,' said the King to his nephew, 'but you must repent and mend your ways.'

'You are no man to reprove me,' said Randolph, 'for your war against the King of England is the crafty hen-raid of a fox rather than the open battle of a true knight.'

'Maybe the time for open battle will come soon enough,' said the King, 'and since you are so keen on it I'll see you get your fill of it. But meantime you are a proud, arrogant boy who doesn't know what he's talking about, and doesn't even know right from wrong, or where his true duty is.'

And the King sent him into confinement until he came to his senses.

RANDOLF   Azure, 3 mullets Argent.

Castles Fall to the King

AFTER the King had dealt with his impudent nephew Randolph, he decided it was time he paid off his long-standing score against his arch-enemy, John of Lorne, that cruel and unscrupulous traitor. So he mustered his army and marched at once for Lorne country.

Long before they got there, John of Lorne's spies warned him of their coming, and he got together an army of about 2000 men from all sides, and sent them to stop the Bruce. They chose a narrow defile which the King's men had to pass through, a place so narrow that two men could scarcely ride abreast through it. On one side was a sheer drop to the craggy rocks of the seashore, and on the other was a steep cliff buttressing a mountain, Ben Cruachan. The River Awe flowed nearby. In this place, dangerous enough in itself, Lorne planted his ambush, taking good care that he himself was aboard his galley on the sea near the Pass of Awe.

But Bruce knew his man and that he was subtle and treacherous as a wolf, and his vigilance was constantly alert for traps. It was obvious to him that this pass was an invitation to his enemies, so he halted. He knew that he must go by the defile, there was no other way, but he considered what to do about the dangers. He then split his army into two parts, the archers under the good James Douglas, the in-fighters staying with him. Douglas then led his men up the mountain-side and perched themselves among the rocks at the top of the cliff over the pass. At a signal, Bruce and his men then marched on, right into the pass, as if unthinkingly. Lorne's men raised their war-cry and rushed out upon them, some of them hurling rocks down from vantage-points up the less sheer parts of the cliff. These did little damage, so cumbersome they were, bounding over into the seashore, and Bruce sent some of his nimbler men swarming up to dislodge the enemy, chasing them out of their holes.

Douglas and his men rained arrows down on the enemy from above, then rushed down to join the mêlée below, where Bruce and his troops were now heavily engaged with the enemy. The men of Lorne fought manfully and well, but when they saw that their supposed advantage had been turned against them, and lacking their cowardly leader to stiffen their resistance, soon became demoralised and fled. Now was Bruce's chance and he rode swiftly upon them with terrible ferocity and slew every man he got within sword-reach. He chased them right to the edge of the River Awe, which ran strong, wide and deep and could be crossed nowhere but at a small bridge downstream a bit from the path. Here the men of Lorne made swiftly for the bridge and, once over, tried to break it down. Bruce's vanguard held it safe, however, till the King himself and all his men got across. Many of the Lorne faction were slain. John of Lorne himself could see it all from the ship, and great was his rage and frustration at the sight.

Bruce took full advantage of his victory over the men of Lorne, and quickly despoiled the whole land of everything seizable, taking a marvellous haul of cattle. Then he trooped swiftly on to Dunstaffnage and laid determined siege to it. This Dunstaffnage Castle stands on a peninsula where Loch Etive meets the sea, and it was the scene of story and legend, including that of Deirdre and the Sons of Uisneach, and the capital of the Scottish kings until 878, when King Kenneth MacAlpin removed the Stone of Destiny, the Liana Fail, from it to Scone in Perthshire, whence it was stolen by Edward I of England and taken to Westminster. It was a stronghold of the Lord of the Isles and passed from the great Somerled to the MacDougalls of Argyll and thence to Lorne. To conquer it, therefore, was the key to Bruce's subjugation of Lorne and his highlanders, and he now attacked it with such utter ferocity that in no time he weakened the garrison's morale and brought about its surrender. He put a good warden in it and supplied it richly with men and victuals so that it would have little difficulty in holding out against attack.

Sir Alexander of Argyll was quick to see the invincibility of Bruce and lost no time in doing homage to him for the sake of his lands. But his son, John of Lorne, was as implacable as ever and escaped by the sea. The whole of Argyll was now effectively in the King's peace, and Bruce returned to Perth for some well-earned recreation.

Many important castles still were held by the English, however: Lothian, Linlithgow, Edinburgh and Stirling among them, and of these Linlithgow Peel was a place of refuge for the English travelling between Edinburgh and Stirling with arms and foodstuffs, and a nuisance to the King. I now propose to recount to you some tales of the taking of certain of these peels and castles still in English hands, Linlithgow foremost among them.

There was a certain farmer called William Bunnock who used to cart hay to Linlithgow Peel. He was a sturdy man of his hands, and honourably worried by the oppression his country suffered under the English occupation. Being a man of fighting temper and burly strength, he was anxious to do something about it, and so were certain friends of his nearby. Bunnock conceived a plan to take the peel, and talked it over with his friends. His idea was that next time he took a load of hay to the peel, his friends would lie in ambush near the castle-gate. Under the hay on his cart, eight of them, well armed, would lie waiting the signal from him to attack: Bunnock himself and another man would walk beside the cart to guide the oxen, each with arms concealed on them. And when the cart was half-way through the gate, Bunnock would shout CALL ALL, CALL ALL! and at this the other man would cut the traces binding the oxen to the cart with a concealed sharp axe, jamming the cart in the gate. The men in the cart would then leap out and join the attack, while the men in the ambush rushed up to support this vanguard.

It was harvest time, the fields broad and heavy with ripe corn and other grains, the trees heavy with fruit. The men of the peel had cut and stacked their hay, and had engaged Bunnock to bring it in, as usual. Bunnock had agreed, laughingly assuring them that this year he would bring a greater and finer load than they had ever seen. And indeed he did, for that night he prepared his men and had the ambush set under cover of darkness, and at the crack of dawn he himself set his wagon rolling towards the peel. Some men had come out from the peel already to work in the fields, which reduced the number within. All went as planned. Bunnock shouted the arranged signal as soon as the wagon was lodged in the gateway, felled the porter who had opened the gate with a terrible blow that shed blood and brains on the cobbles, and helped out the men under the hay. The men in ambush rushed out at once, and soon all were at grips with the castle garrison. After some hard but short fighting the Scots took the castle and slew every man in it. The men in the fields tried to flee, but though some got away to Edinburgh and Stirling, most were slain.

Thus it was that a Scots peasant struck a blow for Scotland, unaided by professional men-at-arms, and when the King came to receive the castle from him, right worthily he rewarded this noble fellow. Bruce then had the whole peel razed to the ground, and took as many men of the district into his peace as could be got to come into it.

He then sent for his nephew, Thomas Randolph, who had been left to gather his thoughts in confinement, and had a good straight talk with him. Randolph had come to his senses meantime, and when the King generously offered him the Earldom of Moray and other lands as a heritage, he wholeheartedly threw in his lot with his noble uncle, and henceforth served faith-

fully at his side. He was a man of mettle, and a great gain for the Scots, and his wisdom, prowess, and unswerving loyalty, once he perceived where his true loyalty belonged, were a mainstay of the King. The King knew his real worth, and that once he gave his word he could be trusted to keep it. I have been told by those who knew him that Randolph was a knight of great qualities, brave, wise, able, and of a noble, indeed kingly, nature. Many great things could be told of him, but I can only relate one of his deeds here, which will be enough to illustrate his character and worth. This is the taking of Edinburgh Castle.

Randolph was a man of middle height, I have been told, of powerful, athletic build, with a broad strong face, a pleasant laugh, and steady bearing. He loved loyalty above all things, honour, generosity and uprightness next, and hated cruelty, falsehood and treason. He had a genuine struggle of conscience over where his true allegiance was, as did many people at this time, including even the King himself. This is because feudalism posited loyalties to foreign overlords, and to a foreign church, which claimed precedence over loyalty to country. The main achievement of the War of Independence was not simply the establishment of the independent throne, but of the nation as the supreme object of one's earthly allegiance. It was a war of nationalism against feudalism, in essence, and few people of the time really understood this, and were genuinely confused in their sense of prior loyalty among conflicting loyalties. To us it is obvious that one's first allegiance is to one's country, but then it was not so. But once Randolph had seen the light, aided by the King's powers of persuasion, his natural virtue made him an unswerving champion of Scotland.

Now that the King and he were again in good relations, Randolph made up for lost time. He put his own lands in order very quickly, and then turned his attentions to doing all he could to help the King free Scotland of the accursed English rule. With the King's consent, he decided to try to take one of the key English strongholds in Scotland, Edinburgh Castle. He took a small body of men quickly to the castle, and laid siege to it. It was a very powerful castle indeed, so strongly built and founded on rock, and so plentifully endowed with stores and men, that it was almost impregnable. In choosing it for his first blow on behalf of his uncle, Randolph showed the real mettle that was in him. He had little hope of taking it easily, but he hoped to be able to wear it down by attrition, harrying the supply lines and starving them out.

The keeper of the castle at that time was Sir Piers Lumbard, a Gascon in the service of the English, and he had once been on talking terms with Bruce. For this reason, when the siege was mounted, his own men suspected him of treason and imprisoned him in the castle, appointing an English constable in his place. This man was very able, and he set about defending the castle with wisdom, energy, vigilance, and cunning skill. And for a long time the siege went on, neither side letting up the pressure. But when news came of Douglas's brilliant seizure of Roxburgh Castle, Randolph grew restive and longed to win a similar glory for himself. Roxburgh, as I shall presently tell you, was won by a subtle trick or stratagem, and Randolph began to think of some such thing for Edinburgh. Trickery went against his noble and forthright grain, but even he could see that this kind of war called for more than just courage and skill in the field. He thought long and hard for some way by which he might take the place, but it seemed impregnable. At last he secretly put word around that any man who should show him a way up the castle rock would be richly rewarded.

Now there was a man called William Francis who had been much about the castle in his boyhood, and, being active and nimble, as well as well mannered and sensible, he had found his own way up the castle cliff. For in his youth he had been in love with a girl in the town and, in order to reach her, he had explored the cliff until he found a place where he could descend. He had made a rope ladder of some twelve feet, the height of the wall at that place, climbed down it, and thence down the cliff and into the town, coming back the same way before dawn. He now offered to lead Randolph and his men up this goat-path to the wall, where they could set up ladders and climb over.

Randolph was delighted at this offer and promised Francis a rich reward for his help. Francis went off and made a ladder of the length he deemed requisite for the purpose, and a night was set for the deed. Taking only thirty men with him, each hand-picked for the necessary qualities, they set out at dead of night in pitch darkness, no moon or stars to glint on any bit of armour that showed beneath their cloaks. It was a dangerous and terrifying climb at the best of times, but in such circumstances you can imagine what it was like. Francis was the only man who knew it well, and he had not done it for years: the others were indeed in the dark, and if any man had fallen, not only would he be broken to pieces on the rocks, but the castle would be alarmed to the presence of the others.

They climbed in grim silence, Francis leading, until they got half-way up, where there was a ledge broad enough for them to sit on. Here they were able to draw breath and rest in preparation for the next half of the climb. But as they sat there, the officers of the watch on the castle above met together just above them, exchanging greetings and reports of their rounds. If they should discover the Randolph party now, in such a situation, no man would escape a horrible death. But the darkness did its work, though there was a moment of breath-taking alarm when an officer looked over the parapet and called out 'Ahah, I spy you there!' and threw down a stone. But he was merely joking with his friends, who laughed at the joke, and the stone missed the party altogether. The watch passed on, quietly talking, and silence fell again. Then Randolph and his men started the climb again, the most dangerous part of all, but all came at last safely to the grassy slope under the wall. Here they set up the ladder, which had been carefully pulled up on a rope after them, stage by stage, and Francis led the way over it, Sir Andrew Gray and Randolph himself close behind. Then the men came up fast, so fast indeed that they made too much noise, and by the time half of them were over, the watch had been alarmed and rushed to investigate. A fierce fight then followed, the watch crying 'Treason! Treason!' and Randolph and his men fighting like madmen. Some of the garrison fled, and in their panic jumped over the wall to a terrible death below. The constable fought well, but he and his men were soon overborne, though they far outnumbered the Scots. Those of the garrison who had been asleep were at a disadvantage, and by the time they had buckled on arms the best of the guard had been slain, thus further demoralising the surprised sleepers. Yet a great resistance was put up, swords ran blood to the hilt, men shrieked and groaned and dreadful was the clamour that thus broke the night. The constable was slain, and the loss of their leader further demoralised his men, and they broke and fled. Randolph himself had been in great danger from the constable and was lucky to escape with his life. But the whole castle was taken, and Randolph triumphed there that night. It is one of the most remarkable captures of a castle I have ever heard of, comparing favourably with that of Alexander at Tyre, where Alexander alone achieved miracles of valour, until his men came up over the walls on ladders.

An interesting fact about this capture is that Malcolm Canmore's sainted Queen Margaret had foreseen it all, back in the eleventh century. For she caused to be engraved on the wall of her chapel, which can still be seen in Edinburgh Castle, a picture of the castle with a ladder standing against the wall, with a man climbing up it: and under the picture she had engraved in French 'Gardez vous de Francois'. And men thought that it meant that the French would so take the castle – but it was Francis, not the French, who took it, and the real meaning there was 'beware of Francis'.

Randolph and his men now searched the castle, seizing all goods and gear. They found Sir Piers Lumbard sitting in fetters and gyves in the dungeon, and he was set free by Randolph, and at once sought to be taken into the King's peace. Word of the great conquest was taken to Bruce, who was overjoyed at his nephew's prowess and proof of his sterling merit. Randolph then caused the castle to be razed so that it could never again easily shelter the English enemy, and received the homage of many men of the surrounding district into his peace on behalf of the King. And worthily the King rewarded his valiant nephew.

The inspiration that fired Randolph at Edinburgh was, as I have said, the taking of Roxburgh by Douglas. The good Sir James was still in the Forest, encamped at Lintalee above Jedburgh and Roxburgh. Many deeds of daring done there I must pass over, being unsure of my information, but this one I do know about. Knowing that Roxburgh could not be taken except by stealth and stratagem, Douglas had been exercising his mind to think out a plot that would deliver the castle into his hands. By and by he got a man called Sim, of the Leadhouse, a very skilful craftsman, to make ladders of hemp rope, with wooden struts across for steps, bound strong enough to take punishing treatment. To each of these was strongly attached a large iron hook of a sort that would hold a firm grip of any battlement it was fixed on.

When these were ready, Douglas got about sixty of his men together, and on Shrove Tuesday they made under cover of darkness to the castle walls. Their armour was covered by black cloaks, and when they came near to the walls, they sent all the horses back and crept along the path in single file, like cows or oxen that had been left out to find their own way home. This was as well, for despite the inky blackness of the night, one of the garrison made out the vague figures and said to his companion, 'That farmer must be hitting the bottle tonight, for he has left his oxen out.' 'Yes,' replied the other, 'and serve him right if Douglas rustles the lot.' And laughingly they went their ways again.

Douglas, who had heard the remarks, sped swiftly to the walls as soon as they had passed. Sim of Leadhouse was able to shin up the wall, and he got up and began to fix the ladders quietly, the men below pulling tight to fix the hooks as he placed them. But he was just fixing a ladder when the man pulling caused it to clank against the stone, and immediately one of the guard came running along. Sim slipped over the edge on to the ladder, hoping neither he nor it would be seen, but the man came right to the spot and looked over. Sim immediately struck upwards with his knife into the man's heart, at the same time grabbing for his throat to prevent a cry escaping. None else seemed to have heard, and Sim threw the body down to the men below, and went on with his task. Men were already swarming up the ladders already fixed, but Sim was spotted yet again while they were climbing, and the guard rushed at him, only to end as his fellow had done. Thus did gallant Sim defend the battlement that night.

Douglas and his men got safely over the wall and made straight for the tower. This being a festival occasion, the garrison were all in the hall dancing, singing and enjoying themselves before the long fast of Lent began next day, believing themselves to be perfectly safe. Then suddenly the cry rang out, 'a Douglas, a Douglas!' and the hall was swarming with Douglas's men slaying with merciless ferocity. Now the garrison outnumbered the Douglas men, but thus caught off guard and unarmed they had no chance, and they fled hither and thither in demoralised panic. The warden of the castle, seeing the way things were going, escaped with as many men as he could muster to the inner tower and closed the gate. Everybody outside it was either slain or captured except for a few who escaped over the walls into the forest.

Next day, the warden, Cylmyne de Fiennes, held out in the tower with stubborn and hopeless tenacity, under a hail of arrows from the attackers. At last, being himself badly wounded in the face and fearing for his life, he surrendered the tower on condition that he and all who were with him were allowed to travel safely into England. Douglas accepted this and had them safely convoyed as far as the English border. But de Fiennes never recovered from the wound and died soon after.

Douglas now sent word to the King via Sim Leadhouse, the hero of the occasion, and greatly the Bruce rewarded him. The valiant Sir Edward Bruce was then sent to Roxburgh to destroy the castle, which he did, leaving scarcely a stone upon stone. And he stayed in the district until all of Teviotdale except Jedburgh and one or two other places near the English border came into the King's peace. He then fought battles farther afield and brought the whole of Galloway and Nithsdale into the King's peace, then took Rutherglen and then Dundee. Great was the might of Sir Edward and few could stand against him. Then, flushed with success, he laid siege to Stirling Castle, the last serious stronghold of the English in Scotland. This was in the keeping of Sir Philip the Mowbray, and he defended it so stoutly that the Scots could not take it. The long war of attrition irked Sir Edward's fiery temperament, for it needed patience rather than action. So when at last the English garrison's supplies beginning to fail, the Mowbray suggested that if King Edward did not relieve the castle by midsummer of the following year, 1314, he would yield it, Sir Edward agreed. He and Sir Philip gave their solemn word of honour on this covenant, and both were knights of honour. So the siege was raised and Sir Edward went to tell the King the glad news.

The Eve of Bannockburn

SIR EDWARD told the King of his covenant with Mowbray, with as much pride as if he had just won a battle instead of throwing the whole campaign, and Scotland, into the greatest danger of the war. The King was appalled and furious at the news. 'What idiocy can have prompted you to such utter folly!' he exclaimed. 'Do you realise what you have done? You've given the English a whole year to prepare a colossal army to come against us and committed not only your own but my honour to meet it in pitched battle. King Edward now has the whole of England, Ireland, Wales and Acquitane, as well as our Scottish enemies, to draw upon, and the wealth to pay such a force. We will be hopelessly outnumbered both in men and arms. All that we have struggled to build up is now to be hazarded in a gamble that only an act of God can turn our way!'

'Let the King of England marshal his whole people down to the very schoolboys against us,' Sir Edward replied, 'yet, as God is my witness, we will give them a lesson they will never forget, even if they were as many again!'

And angry though he was, the King could not but admire the great spirit thus manifested by his impetuous brother. 'So be it, brother,' he said, relenting, 'and since there's no help for it now, let us too prepare manfully for this final trial of worth with the English. Let every true Scot who loves the freedom of his nation beyond all things prepare himself for the coming battle with all the force he can muster, so that if our enemies indeed try to relieve Stirling we will thwart their aim.'

This was agreed upon, and all true Scots were fired with excitement at the prospect of the coming severe trial, and every one prepared himself in every way for the day that was coming. The whole country became a training camp and arms factory.

Meanwhile King Edward, having heard the news from Sir Philip the Mowbray, was overjoyed at the obvious folly of the Scots in giving him such an incredible chance of winning Scotland for ever. He can be forgiven if he thought that Bruce was the greatest general who ever snatched defeat from the jaws of victory. And there was much laughter and joking about the folly of the Scots among the English nobles as they prepared themselves for the coming massacre of Bruce's little army under the English juggernaut of war. But they did not know that quite a little stone can overturn a very big wagon, nor did they think that God decides issues otherwise than they would seem to go.

The English too prepared for the coming trial, and King Edward raised the biggest army the country had ever seen. He had men from many foreign countries, great knights who had no real interest in the Scottish war, but were merely playing the feudal game which took no thought of nationhood, and still less of the rights of the peoples. He had a whole company of French knights, professional brawlers who cared as little for England as they did for Scotland, but were always ready to enrich themselves by a bit of plunder easily come by, and others of the same breed from various other parts of Europe. The whole of English chivalry were mustered, down to the gray-beards who could do little more than heave a cutlass, and some of the best of

Wales, Ireland, and the Scottish traitors. It is said that altogether over 30,000 fighting men took the road to Bannockburn against the Scots – a match which makes David's duel with Goliath seem child's play. There were 12,000 horsemen alone, and of these fully a thousand were in full armour, both horse and man covered with steel, for the heavy cavalry vanguard: 15,000 archers, an undeclared number of light-armed horsemen, and a vast army of camp-followers and servants of both horse and man. Great trains of wagons filled with supplies were prepared to carry tents, utensils, furnishings, food, ammunition, fuel, and all the other necessities of an army on the march. So huge was the host that took the fateful road to Scotland that they stretched on all sides from horizon to horizon, a vast sea of waving banners, flashing armour, neighing horses, helmets and shields, so that it must have seemed that not even God and all His congregated might of angels could have prevailed against it.

Such was the army that came in due course to Berwick, where they camped for a time in and about the town. King Edward, seeing his huge army in excellent spirits, was so exultant that he felt there wasn't a king anywhere in the world could stand against such an army. He planned to subjugate the whole of Scotland and parcel out the land among his own men: he was a very generous chap with other people's property, and his men boasted about what they would do to the Scots. But they reckoned without their host, and the mantle of their pride was to be torn and tattered.

King Edward, on the advice of his generals, divided his men into ten battalions, each of 3000 men, all determined to fight to the death and leave no item of spoil in the hands of the Scots. Each battalion had a picked general over it, and the Earls of Gloucester and Hereford led the first two of them, with many fine captains under their command. They were all men of proven ability and they had an overweening conviction of their own invincibility.

And having thus arranged his followers, King Edward himself took one battalion with the valiant knight Sir Giles d'Argentine as his aide on one side of him and Sir Aymer de Valence, Earl of Pembroke, on the other. These two men he esteemed above all others, despite Sir Aymer's setbacks in Scotland.

It was therefore in fine battle order that the vast English army set out one sunny morning from Berwick on the last lap of their journey. They covered whole hills and valleys, the broad battalions riding over countryside ten abreast, and each battalion several men deep. The sun shone clear and bright, striking fire from burnished helm and shield and blinding breast-plate, the proud banners blazing, pennons flapping in the breeze, so many and varied in colour and device that words fail me, and the whole countryside was aflame with life and colour.

They came thus soon to Edinburgh, the whole population of Scotland scarcely greater in number and infinitely poorer in gear and gain.

King Robert, as usual, had spent the time he had in studying the ground of the impending battle. He had one supreme advantage to offset the English overall vast superior strength – that in the coming duel it was he who chose, if not the weapons, the ground for the fight: and we have seen how Bruce could make the very soil worth thousands of fighting men, how he could make the terrain of Scotland fight for its own integrity. And when he heard of the coming of so vast an English army on to Scottish soil, he called together all his men at a place called the Torwood, near Stirling, but a few miles in front of the castle, where a burn called the Bannock ran through swampy ground to join the River Forth to the east of the castle. Sir Edward Bruce was there with a fine army of his own mustering; Walter the Steward of Scotland, still only a boy with fledgling beard, with a noble warrior-band of his own; the good Sir James Douglas with his veteran guerilla troops; Randolph,

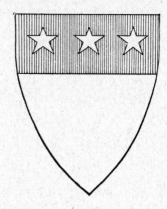

Earl of Moray, with his men still fresh from the triumphant capture of Edinburgh; and many other veteran troops well tried and unlikely to be easily frightened by mere numbers.

But it is not to be thought that there was any delusion among the Scots about the plight they were in. King Robert was being forced to do what he had always gone out of his way to avoid – meet the superior English armies in pitched battle. His policy, which has been called *Good King Robert's Testament*, was a strategy of guerilla raids, scorched-earth retreats to deprive advancing armies of victuals, constant harrying of supply lines, stealthy night attacks on camps and castles, and the destruction of all castles taken lest they give further shelter to the enemy. It is a strategy which has become time-honoured, and has won country after country its independence, best suited to a small country with only a folk-army of the determined citizenry and peasants, under occupation by a powerful enemy. It was essentially a policy of defence, of driving out an invader. Now he must reverse it and put his whole campaign to the hazard of one pitched battle in which all the odds except one, the choice of terrain, were stacked against him. All this the Scots knew well.

When the King's army had fully assembled it numbered, I am told, some 10,000 men, not counting the small folk and non-fighting army services. They were not only numerically inferior to the English but were very much less well accoutred, though in human quality each man was more than a match for his English opposite number. The King inspected them all, examined their equipment, and satisfied himself on their high morale, which is more important than anything else in an army. His practised eye noted the boldness of stance, the glint of purpose in the eye, the set of the mouth, the air of quiet but grim resolution of a people that has stood all it can stand from an oppressor and is determined to be free or die. With such men in such a frame

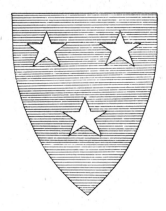

of mind, he thought, the miracle may indeed be achieved. Everywhere he went the same air of resolution impressed him and greatly raised his own heart to the coming battle; manner, word, gesture, appearance, everything bespoke no ordinary army playing a war game, but grim men knowing that everything they love and care for in this world is at stake. Never was a king so rejoiced in his people, nor a people so fulfilled in a king; for Bruce, as he rode among them, was the very incarnation of the spirit of Scottish manhood and resistance to intolerable oppression. Thus King and people inspired each other, and the general tone of the army was raised to a height rarely equalled in history, and surpassed, if at all, only by the Spartans at Thermopylae.

Greatly heartened, King Robert called a council of war and addressed his nobles thus:

'Gentlemen, you see now how the English have come in great strength and battle order to relieve that castle over there, according to their word. Therefore we must now set our own armies in order and decide how best to deploy them. We have a good 10,000 men at our disposal, and I propose to make four battalions of them. It is almost certain that the enemy will have to march by the New Park, for they cannot cross the marshes of the Carse, and that is where I propose to meet them. On the east side will be the Pows with its swampy streams running across the Carse to the Forth, and on the west is the forest and the hills. They will have to cross the burn near Bannock, which will be a difficult business for their heavier troops, and there I propose to attack them. We shall use their own weight and strength against them, and use it to overthrow them. They will meet us with heavy cavalry and infantry with long powerful spears. The ground will sink under their sheer weight, so we will help them to sink even further by riddling it with potholes and ditches with calthrops in them to disable the horses. They have aimed at impregnable solidity, so we will aim at lightning mobility. By swift and accurate switching of troops from one point to another it will be possible for us to make up

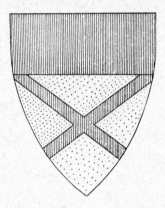

for our lack of numbers. We will cut the ground from under their feet, sink them in confusion, and slay them where they stand bogged down in their own weight of arms.'

This plan was welcomed by the council, and the four battalions were at once set up under Randolph, Sir Edward Bruce, Walter the Steward aided by Douglas (they were cousins) because of his youth, and the King himself. Bruce's men were from his own Carrick, Argyll, and the Isles, with a host of lowlanders as well. This powerful battalion he proposed to use as a rearguard, the shaft of a spear-head consisting of a vanguard with the flanks formed by the other three battalions. This allowed Bruce to general the battle keeping a sharp eye on all that was going on from raised ground in the rear sending in men from his own battalion wherever they were most needed all up and down the battle-line. This shows the wisdom of the King, for on such good generalship depends the real outcome of battle – a leader in the press of fighting has no idea what is going on elsewhere, and cannot conduct the fighting. It was the very lack of such wise generalship which was the undoing of the English. Randolph and his battalion were placed to the north end of the line, at Kirkton St. Ninians; Stewart and Douglas were the southern flank; and Sir Edward Bruce, as befits his status and character, had the honour of leading the vanguard.

Thus everything was set for the battle, and the King and his men camped next day, Saturday, in the New Park, while the English lay at Edinburgh. The approach which Bruce reckoned the English must take, coming from Falkirk to Stirling, was thoroughly mined with pits and calthrops, so close together that they were like a honeycomb, covered with green turf to delude the enemy. As at Loudoun Hill, Bruce created a bottle-neck through which the enemy troops were forced to decant in comparatively small numbers, so that they had no chance to use their sheer weight of numbers – the ditches and pits, the woods and swamps hemmed them into a narrow pass. The King as usual had planned the battle like a master-general, which he was. Before the battle began he was in almost complete control not only of his own men but of the enemy also, thanks to his planning genius: the battle was fought and won in his brilliant mind before it ever began.

Bannockburn–the First Day

ON THE Sunday morning of 23rd June 1314, soon after sunrise, which was about 3 a.m. that day, the Scots all gathered to say mass, kneeling bareheaded, and devoutly shriving themselves. Each man was determined to win or die for Scotland and his own that day, for the freedom of his family and his people. They fasted all day in keeping with the religious discipline for the feast of St. John the Baptist, whose day it was. The King then rode all over the prepared ground, carefully checking that everything was as it should be, every turf in its place over the pits with their deadly calthrops inside, the road so hemmed about with pits and ditches that a narrow bottleneck was made to constrict the cavalry and let only a reduced number through at a time. He then gave orders for the army to get into proper array, every man thoroughly accoutred ready for the order to take up positions. Randolph was specially briefed to guard the road past the Kirk of St. Ninians, where Bruce feared a breakaway body of English cavalry might, by riding northeast from the main approach, outflank his army altogether and come into Stirling by that route. If they tried such a move, Randolph was to throw in his swiftest schiltrom and stop them head-on.

The King then made it known that any man who wanted to leave could do so now, but their ardent response made him exult in his heart at their courage, sure that an army of such exceptional and inspiring morale could indeed achieve miracles of valour. The small folk he sent to stand by with their home-made arms in a valley behind Coxet Hill, out of sight of the enemy.

Scouts reported that the enemy were marching from Falkirk in magnificently impressive order: Bruce suppressed this information from the other ranks, lest it disturb their excellent morale, and put it about that the enemy were ill-disciplined and straggling. Not expecting pitched battle, but only some skirmishing on this Sunday, the King himself watched the approach to the New Park, letting Douglas and Sir Edward keep the rear, with Moray posted in his proper place to guard the kirk road. Sir Robert Keith, who had been put in charge of the 500 or so light cavalry which Bruce kept in readiness and the utmost mobility to relieve where most needed, was sent to spy on the advancing English. It was they who saw the full might of the English army flashing in the sunlight, and sent news to the King of its impressive might, which he very properly suppressed. He ordered the scouts to go about among the men jeering at the English disorder, themselves making great show of confidence. There are times when propaganda has greater value than the strict truth, and this was one of them, and never did the King show greater leadership than in this matter. He himself went among the men with bold and resolute bearing, inspiring them with all the confidence he could. Then he

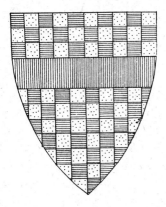

went back to his front-line position to the south of Douglas, to watch the advance.

When they were about two miles distant from the Scottish army, the English halted and sent a division of heavy cavalry under Lord Clifford off to the east to outflank the Scots altogether and come at the castle by the kirk road, guarded by Randolph. The King saw this and, after watching for a time, saw no counter-move being made by Randolph. He at once despatched a messenger to him with the rebuke that Randolph was letting a rose fall from the chaplet of his good fame. Randolph at once sent his strongest schiltrom of close-knit long-spearmen against the English. This schiltrom formation was the basic infantry technique used by the Scots under Wallace at Falkirk, and ever since. It had two main manœuvres – it could attack as a long close-knit line, or it could defend as a packed tight wall of spears. The latter deployment could withstand a heavy cavalry charge, for the horses came to grief on the wall of spears: then the former could be used to press

home the advantage on the unhorsed and confused knights. Randolph had
lost valuable time, but by making double speed he managed to get ahead of
the English on the road and turned his men to face them, in the defence
formation. Great was the courage needed by these veteran spearmen to face
the appalling charge of the English cavalry, but there was not the least sign
of wavering. Sir William Dayncourt and Sir Thomas Grey led the charge,
bold men of their hands. Sir William charged without stopping right into the
schiltrom and both he and his horse were immediately killed. Seeing this,
Sir Thomas tried to rein up at the last moment, but was thrown from his
horse, seized by some of the schiltrom and taken prisoner. The rest of the
charging English drew rein and approached the hedgehog of spears more
warily, to see if they could find a way to break through. They surrounded
the Scots and drove at them in short sallies which were easily repulsed,
Randolph's men severely wounding the horses and slaying their riders when
they fell. Frustrated and furious, the remaining English vanguard hurled
maces, battle-axes and even swords at the Scots to try to break a way through,
but they ended up only as spoil and did little damage. Yet the sheer number
and weight of the English pressed the Scots hard, and it was tiring work
hurling back these great tanks of horses. The heat of the day was no help, and
soon the Scots were pouring sweat and tiring badly, while the great clouds
of dust and stour raised by the trampling hooves of horses and feet of men
made it difficult to see. Manfully as they fought, things began to look bad for
the Scots. James Douglas, who was riding freely that day, came to Bruce and
asked permission to go at once to Randolph's assistance. Bruce, however, was
adamant. 'I am not going to break up my plans because of Randolph's in-
competence. He's done enough damage already.' But Douglas persisted and
the King relented. There was no time to lose, so Douglas made off at double
speed.

No sooner had he gone than one of the most notable incidents of the battle
occurred. Bruce, not expecting full pitched battle that day, was riding about
lightly armed on a small palfrey, taking stock of the terrain, keeping an eye
on the enemy formation, making last checks on his own defences and plans,
with particular eye to the terrain. The English army had halted very near,
but the vanguard, not knowing this, rode on towards the Scots in New Park.
Bruce drew up his troops in battle order, seeing this, and rode out in front to
inspect them. He wore only a leather hat on his head, surmounted by his own
personal coronet.

Now there was a young knight of great promise in the English vanguard,
Sir Henry de Bohun, who was nephew to the Earl of Hereford, Humphrey
de Bohun, Constable of England. The vanguard did not know that Sir
Philip the Mowbray had already told King Edward that there was no need

for him to fight the Scots at all, as the pact he had made with Edward Bruce stated that if an English army came to Stirling, the castle would be considered relieved. King Edward, in his overweening pride, had dismissed this wise advice anyway, but it is typical of the lack of overall generalship of the English army that his vanguard were not halted and informed. And now a further act of vainglory showed the want of good order and military discipline on the English side. For this Henry de Bohun, more concerned with his own personal ambitions than with what might be his commander's will, saw a chance to win great renown for himself by killing the lightly armed Bruce before the battle began. It was a stupid and foolhardy notion, of doubtful valour if one thinks of the unequal mounting of the two men, and of still more doubtful wisdom when one considers the proven greatness of Bruce. This de Bohun was fully armed on a big charger (also fully armed), and with a twelve-foot lance in his hand. Now, on the impulse, he couched his lance and charged straight at the King. For a moment Bruce was slightly incredulous at the folly of it, then saw the daring behind the impulse, and the foolhardiness, from which he guessed it was a young and headstrong knight who came against him. He saw also that his handling of this matter would be carefully watched by his own army. Now Bruce had been taught as a young squire how to deal with such an attack, and many a time had stood on foot with nothing but a three-foot stick in his hand as his old instructor or jousting opponent came riding down full pelt upon him with muffled lance: sometimes he had sat on the wooden training-horse and stood the attack that way. And as he saw de Bohun come at him, he remembered many a buffet he had received and given in that early training, and the technique of striking the lance behind the head as it approached, in a back-handed swinging stroke, and following through a circular movement to bring the stick or sword crashing down on the lancer as he passed. It was a stroke he had used many a time in the past, though not for many a long year. The importance of the opportunity this gave him to inspire his own men and demoralise the foe was not lost on him.

All this must have flashed through his mind as, instead of retreating behind his troops, he rode out to meet the advancing lancer. As the distance between them shortened, de Bohun crouched low behind his lance, and put his horse full out. Bruce, who carried only a battle-axe, flexed his axe-arm and measured the stroke in his mind. Then de Bohun was on him. As the lance-point came quivering near, Bruce touched his palfrey to the left, and swerved in the saddle, at the same time striking back at the lance with the back of his axe, and, following the stroke through, rose in his stirrups at the top of the stroke and aimed at de Bohun's helmet. The force of the stroke, the speed of the charger, the weight of the impact, sent the axe-blade sheering through

steel and into bone and brain, so that the axe was wrenched from the King's hand. De Bohun reeled and slowly fell from his horse, and the King rode back and detached his axe from the cleft skull. The shaft of it had broken with the impact, and the strength of the King's grip on it.

This was the first stroke of the battle of Bannockburn, and it symbolised for both sides the whole battle itself. It showed how a heavy, headlong, ill-disciplined and leaderless enemy can be overcome by men thoroughly trained, seasoned, hardened in grim experience, and of a courage and purpose drawn from deeper sources than mere pride or personal bravado. With that encounter and its outcome, the battle of Bannockburn began as it was to end.

The King rode back to his men with the broken axe in his hand, a proud figure indeed, and every man, except perhaps the most hardened knights who knew only too well that this was a demonstration of a classical stroke learned in the hard school of jousting, was inspired by the great prowess of their King. The common soldiers saw in him an almost godlike leader of almost superhuman powers. The more experienced knights, however, took the King to task for thus unnecessarily risking his own life, and with it the success of the whole campaign and the freedom of Scotland. They saw it as a needless risk, for although they all knew the technique for dealing with such an attack, and many of them could just as easily have demonstrated it, it seemed to them a piece of showing off on the King's part which, if it had miscarried, might have cost them the whole war. So they gently upbraided him for this unusual lack of wisdom and good generalship. But all he said was, 'Well, it certainly cost me a good battle-axe.'

The English were no less impressed by the encounter, and the least tried of them started to flee. This, plus the excitement in the Scottish ranks, led to a breach of discipline in the Scots army, for when they saw the English retreat, many charged after them in pursuit, and it was some time before Bruce and his captains could get them back under control. The King was certainly to blame for much of this, and it was unlike him: but the peculiar circumstances and the psychological effect it had on both sides perhaps justified it, who knows?

Randolph, during all this, was still hard pressed on the St. Ninian's road, but Douglas and his men soon came up. This demoralised the English, who began to give way, and Douglas saw that there was no real need to throw in his men, thus depriving Randolph of the full credit for victory, which would go a long way to put him right with the King for failing to head them off in time. So the noble Douglas held his hand and his men, letting Randolph take full credit for the victory. Randolph and his men, seeing the English falter, redoubled their strokes and soon had utterly routed the enemy. Then at last the Scots were able to cast off their helmets and armour and let the air get at their sweat-drenched bodies. And anyone who saw them there, panting like exhausted horses, worn and weary with hard fighting, would not have needed telling that these men had just proved their worth in battle. Everybody was overjoyed that Randolph had thus recovered his fallen rose, and so covered himself in glory. But the King said nothing for a while, looking thoughtfully at the ground as the knights gathered round Randolph congratulating him. Then he began to speak.

'Gentlemen,' he said, 'let us thank God for allowing us a lucky start to this business. The effect of two such defeats thus early on our enemies is not to be underestimated. For when the main body of their troops hear how we have dealt with their vanguard and heavy cavalry, the best men they have got, their morale will take a serious blow. Their hearts will fail them, and if the heart fails, the body is worthless, no matter how bulky it may be. Therefore I have faith that from so auspicious a beginning a successful outcome will follow. Nevertheless, I have been thinking seriously of the wisdom of this battle. I myself want to fight, but there is so much at stake that I feel I want the decision whether or not to fight to be yours rather than mine. Our honour has already been vindicated. So has Mowbray's and King Edward's. The terms of the pact are already fully met, so there is no necessity for us to take on hand so perilous a battle. My instinct has been from the start to wear the English down by constant guerilla harrying, for we do not seek to conquer them but only to make them leave us alone and get out of Scotland, and avoid pitched battles. I am still of this mind, though I would dearly like to fight them now, come what may, if I had only myself to think of. But the cause is greater than any one of us. Therefore I would like to hear your counsel, which you may speak forthrightly and plainly, and I promise, to abide by your will.'

The nobles stood silent for a moment, and looked at each other. Then, as if by common unspoken consent, one of them, I know not who, said 'Sire, your goodness and wisdom are deeply moving, but our will is that as soon as the day breaks to-morrow you give order for battle. We will not fail you through fear of death or any effort that is necessary to make our country free once again.'

The King was delighted by this manly and spontaneous response, for he had indeed been unwilling to put the whole campaign and all that it had achieved to the test of one pitched battle against such huge odds, and only his honour had forced him to it after his brother had committed him. But his pride and sense of the possibility of a great victory urged him to fight, and this declaration greatly heartened him. So he said, 'Well, since you would have it so, gentlemen, prepare at once to have mass said before sunrise, each man in battle array, with all banners displayed. See to it that no man breaks ranks, and, as you love me, I beg you to get yourselves each a good standard-bearer and, when it comes to the fight, set heart and sinew to break the over-weening arrogance of the enemy. They will have great strength of cavalry and hurl it at you full speed. Let your schiltroms stand firm behind their spears and avenge upon them the great wrongs that they and theirs have done us, and will do again if they can.

'And truly, when one thinks of it, we have every reason to be undismayed and valiant, for we have three great advantages over them. The first is moral, for there can be no doubt that right is on the side of a people that fights to free itself from a foreign yoke: and every man worth his salt will fight for the right. The next is economic, for we are hungry and an impoverished nation and they have brought with them here into our own lands such wealth of gear and valuables that if we win, as under God we may well do, each man will so benefit that the poorest of you will be both rich and influential. And the third advantage is necessity, for whereas they come here only out of arrogant wilfulness trusting to subdue us by sheer weight of arms, we fight only because we must. We have no real choice but to fight for our lives, our families, and the freedom of Scotland, whereas they seek to destroy us because they despise us. But they will get more than they bargain for, whatever the outcome.

'And to this matter of necessity I might add a warning that if they win, which God forbid, they will treat us with the most merciless cruelty. You all know this as well as I do, for you've had your fill of the English rule in Scotland. Therefore let every man set himself to fight with all the dour strength he can summon up and meet the first attackers with such manly valour that there need be no more than first attackers, for the others behind will lose heart. Think of all the good you have ever achieved and the happiness that is within reach if we, as may well be, manage to pull this off. Every one of you will carry, believe me, honour, praise, riches, freedom, and the welfare and happiness of your country in your hands, if you conduct yourselves like men. The opposite will befall you if cowardice and weakness are allowed to betray you. If you had all been willing to live in slavery and subjection you could easily have done so. It is precisely because you longed for freedom above all things that we are here together, and to gain that goal there is nothing for it but to be valiant, strong and undismayed.

'Let me warn you again that no greater ill can become any of us than to fall into the hands of the enemy alive. You know what they did to my brother Neil, and to everybody else who has been taken by them. But when I consider your valour, the many great deeds you have achieved in these campaigns of ours, I am utterly convinced that we shall not only win this battle but be triumphantly victorious. Our enemies have great bulk, it is true, but they are motivated by nothing better than lust for power, they are arrogantly in the wrong, and in their hearts they must know it.

'Now, as to practical matters, you see that this ground is so chosen that we cannot be surrounded, and that, on the contrary, by its very nature and the way we have prepared it, we have rendered the mere superior weight of the enemy more of a liability to him than an advantage. We shall use his own weight to overthrow him. And I beg you all, both officers and men, to put victory before any greedy temptations to grab spoil that may come your way, or to take lucrative prisoners. Resist it utterly until you see that the battle has been indeed won and that the field is ours. Then you may indulge yourselves as much as you like in seizing the rewards you will have so richly earned. If you bear this in mind, victory will certainly be yours.

'I think that is all I have to say. You all know well enough what honour is, and can be trusted to uphold your own, without my telling you. But one thing I faithfully promise every one of you, I swear on my own honour that if any man is killed in this battle, the heir to his estate, no matter how young he may be, will possess his lands from this day forth free of all dues to guardian or overlord. That is my solemn pledge to you. And now let every man prepare for battle, and may God be with us. My advice is to prepare now and rest all night in your armour so that we cannot be taken by surprise.'

And the assembled leaders said in one voice 'So be it!', and they went off to their squadrons and did as he had commanded. Every man armed himself for battle and spent the night on the ground where he was to stand, when the sun rose.

Bannockburn - the Second Day

MEANWHILE Clifford and his savaged cavalry had returned to the English encampment and reported the disaster of their defeat. They told King Edward and his knights of the success of the Scottish schiltrom of spearmen against heavy cavalry, of Bruce's exemplary slaughter of de Bohun, of the death of Dayncourt and the capture of Grey, and all the rest of it. We may be sure that, in order to excuse themselves, they did not underpaint the picture of Scottish ferocity. The result was further and serious undermining of the English morale, and among the ordinary rank and file there were mutterings about their lords leading them into unjust wars of might over right, which is tempting Providence. And when the leaders noticed this disaffection, they conferred among themselves and sent heralds to proclaim that the day's set-backs should not be taken too seriously, that such things happened in mere skirmishes, but that in full battle they could not happen: and that the Scots would pay in full for their petty victories. Therefore, they said, let all Englishmen stand strong in the day's battle and take their revenge.

But lords may exhort, and men seem to respond, but in their hearts the English were troubled and dispirited. A good man cannot give of his best in a bad cause, and the best of them had their doubts about King Edward's cause in Scotland.

The English were afraid of night attack by the Scots, and they spent a restless night down in the swampy Carse, trying to get their main army across the Bannock burn on to firmer ground, under cover of darkness. They broke down whole houses for timber of various sorts to bridge the burn and its tributary 'pows', and it is said that some of the Stirling garrison slunk out to them with supplies of doors and other wooden planking to help in the work. It was a sleepless night for them, but by morning the bulk of the army had got across and was in a stronger position for the battle.

The Scots rested all night in their armour and when day began to break they heard mass, took a light meal, and prepared themselves for battle. Before the battle, as is customary on such momentous occasions, the King visited and inspected his squadrons, making new knights of some of his most tried and trusted leaders. On this occasion he at last knighted the good James of Douglas, Walter Stewart, and several other men of noble achievement, each in his degree. Then they all took up their prearranged positions, set out in order, each troop with its specific part to play in the whole plan of battle, for Bruce left nothing to chance that could possibly be planned ahead. And each man there was dedicated to his country's cause.

Opposite them on the field, the ranks of the English shone like angels, but in a disorderly mass instead of purposeful units like the Scots. The only separate, directable division they had was the vanguard, a great company of heavy cavalry sporting many a brave and famous banner.

When King Edward, who was used to ostentation and pomp, saw the sober, small and light-armed ranks of the Scots, he was astonished. He could

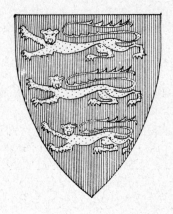

not believe that such a rag-and-bobtail lot as they seemed to be to his luxurious eyes would possibly dare oppose itself to his mighty panoply of armour, mere infantry against the pride of English chivalry. 'What!' he said, 'surely these Scots cannot seriously intend to fight me with such a ragtailed rout?'

'Indeed they do, Sire,' said Sir Ingram de Umphraville, a renegade Scot in Edward's army. 'Yon is the most remarkable sight I have ever seen – a Scottish army at last prepared to give battle in the open instead of making skulking attacks from ambush. I know them, and if you will take my advice, Sire, you will easily win this day. The way to defeat them is suddenly to withdraw, retreat back past our tents as if we had no intention of fighting, and I promise you that you will see that ordered formation break ranks and rush like hungry wolves at our tents to grab the spoil. Then we can round on them and destroy them utterly among the tents.'

'Retreat?' said King Edward, 'As God is my witness no man shall ever

say that I shirked battle with such a rabble, or had to use trickery to defeat them.'

As he spoke, he saw all the Scots kneel down devoutly to pray before the coming battle, and King Edward said to Sir Ingram, 'You see, these people are kneeling to beg for mercy!'

'They do indeed, Sire,' said the disgusted Sir Ingram, 'but not from you. I've given you my advice, and I'll tell you now that these men asking mercy from God will win this battle utterly or die in the attempt. You certainly won't frighten them into flight.'

'So be it then,' said the King, 'we'll soon see who knows best.'

Then he ordered the trumpets to sound the rally, and this was the signal for swift activity on both sides. The Scots were now in proper battle order, Sir Edward Bruce holding the van in the centre, Douglas on the right flank, Randolph on the left, the King with his men and Sir Robert Keith's cavalry holding the rear, ready to send in men fast wherever the press was hardest on the main three divisions. King Robert himself was on a hillock known as the Borestone, with his aides, keeping a sharp watch on every point of his forward divisions.

The English sounded the charge, and at once the heavy cavalry in the van rode powerfully at Sir Edward Bruce and his troops in the vanguard of the Scots. The two sides clashed there with a mighty clatter and splintering of spears, crackling noisily like sparking hot fat, and the din could be heard for miles around.

In that hard clash many a good steed ended on Scottish spears, many a good knight was unseated and slain, many a deed of bold valour was mightily achieved. Foe struck at foe with ill-matched weapons, the wounded horses were allies of Scotland as backward they, maddened, stamped among their own; yet on came the English right boldly into battle. Dourly the Scots met them with spear and battle-axe matched against swords, and sore were the wounds there sustained by many. Stubborn and fierce was the fight at that quarter and many the valiant knight fell to rise no more. Hard effort the Scots called forth to conquer the might of their powerful foes, no pain nor peril too great for their courage till the English laboured in serious trouble.

Randolph, Earl of Moray, nephew of King Robert and hero of St. Ninians only yesterday, closed in beside Sir Edward and met the proud English, his banner waving above the contestants. Hard and determined was the English onslaught, matching the might of armoured horse vainly against the mobile spearmen, now dashing forward, now bunched like a hedgehog, vainly trying to ride down the Scotsmen. Stern and harsh was the fight, bitter the wounds dealt on both sides, blood burst from shoulder and heart, yea, hearts burst under breast-plate, gore gushed through the armour to drench the suffering soil. Randolph and his men so powerfully fought there that soon they gained ground ever more and more over their foes, although they were ten to one. The Scots at times seemed to be bobbing about in a sea of Englishmen. The English, seeing this, charged with all their power, hoping to overwhelm them utterly, but the Scots met them face to face with spear, sword and battle-axe, and hewed them down. It was a mighty struggle so grimly fought there as men exchanged lives, went down to spear, axe, mace, sword, knife or other weapon. Green grass soon ran red with gore as many men fell dead and wounded. Randolph and his men earned lasting fame that day for duty well done upon the foe.

The joining of battle had rather altered the pattern of forces by this time, and Douglas was left comparatively disengaged, so he and young Stewart ran their troops up to help Randolph, making a ferocious assault upon the English with naked steel and driving might of arms. The English fought back as powerfully, and for a time the battle raged grimly without any sign of the outcome, two great forces fighting to the death. So great was the spilling of blood that it now stood in pools on the ground. Great slaughter the Scots made, bore themselves like heroes, and strewed the field with blood. The three divisions were fighting side by side, weapon struck on armour, the air clanged as from a myriad anvils, horses and proud knights went down on all sides, many the ornate and richly coloured garment was trodden deep into mire and gore.

All this time little sound of voice was heard except grunting and panting, with occasional cries or groans of the stricken, but for the most part all saved their breath for the work in hand. Things looked bad for the Scots when the English archers began to pour a rain of death into the air, but Bruce, at once seeing the danger from his vantage-post, ordered Keith and his 500 light cavalry to charge the archers, spit them on their lances or hew them down with swords. Keith charged at once and did such merciless slaughter among the archers, taking no prisoners, that soon they were scattered on all sides once for all. The English trump card had been itself trumped.

Now, however, the Scottish archers in Bruce's division were given their chance, and a hail of arrows sped into the English ranks. Unlike Bruce, Edward had no answer to this menace, and soon the ranks of the English were being thinned out by them. Keith and his men still rode about after the fleeing English archers, slaying every man they could get their weapons on, doing devastating havoc among them, so that the remnant fled in utter panic back to their own lines, demoralising the others. But their flight made room for the second wave of English cavalry, and it joined in the fray. The King saw this and at last sent his own division, which he had held in reserve, into the battle, saying, 'Now, sirs, into battle with you and see that you be valiant and bold, and use your wits. You will turn the tide, for the enemy are now fighting all out, our own men are more than holding their own, and your fresh and powerful pressure will break them. Let hate drive every stroke, for they have given us great cause to hate them, seizing our good lands, oppressing our people, making our goods their own. They have murdered our kin for defending themselves, hanged and drawn our patriots as traitors, and they will destroy us if they can. But God has this day granted us a day of reckoning with them.'

At these words the King's men charged with such force that the English reeled back as from supernatural force. Terrible and merciless was the slaughter, for the Scots fought like men possessed, they laid on like madmen, full of maniacal drive. No armour could stand against the terrible hammer blows they dealt, and it says much for the courage of the English that they stood the punishment as long as they did. Mighty was the din of battle in that place as steel rung upon steel and the ground was torn up underfoot by the trampling, plunging, seething masses of battle-locked men. Battle-cries now tore the air to tatters, horrible was the uproar and dreadful the wounds dealt on all sides.

Powerfully Sir Edward Bruce battled still in the forefront of the fight, his men so bold and invincible, fighting with such skill and purpose, that the English van was broken and gave way. Ignoring the commands of their leaders, they fled back to the main body still waiting their chance to get through the bottle-neck and into the fight. But the main body itself had not long to wait, for the Scots came pressing through and carried the fight to them, Douglas, Stewart, Randolph all covering themselves with glory in that dour fighting. Many a horse ran riderless among the labouring forces, adding to the confusion, and more and more above the battle rose the cry of the Scots, 'On them, upon them! They falter, they fail!'

The sore pressure of the attack, combined with the deadly fire of the Scottish archers, began to tell, and the English fell back, falling more and more into confusion and fear, for they fought as a mob with no real overall leadership, like a body without a head. Not so were the Scots, whose King, as always, conducted his troops like a master of musicians in the concert of war. It was clear that the Scots had already the victory, the English had given their best and their best was not good enough, and now they fell back, and their courage, great in the fight, began to give way to expediency. At this point, while both sides were still manfully contesting the outcome, the small folk who had been left in the hollow behind Coxet Hill now appeared over the hill, having perceived the way it was going, and came with home-made banners of sheets on poles, and spears, to help their lords and share the spoil, a good few thousand of them. They marched resolutely down the hill which was a long enough way from the field for the English not to see clearly what men they were, and the English mistook them for another proper division of troops, and their hearts failed them. When Bruce perceived this (for as ever he was missing no point of the game) he rallied his own men, and raising his own battle-cry, hurled them once more into the fray. The English were now increasingly demoralised and confused, and soon they were fleeing in all directions from the terrible battlemania of the Scots. A hard core of their best men still fought on, for that race were ever stubborn and of high courage in the field, but they were diverted by their weaker fellows, and they dearly bought their honourable stand.

When King Edward saw his men break in various parts of the battle and flee, and the might of the Scots carrying the press against the hard core of his troops so that they fell back defeated before them, he was himself so dismayed that he fled with his company of 500 cavalry in utter disorder, making for Stirling Castle. Thus I have been told, though others have said that the King was led from the field against his will by Sir Aymer de Valence when he saw that all was lost, and the King himself in danger.

Sir Giles de Argentine, that noblest of the English knights, accompanied the King some way from the battlefield, then said, 'Sire, I have done my duty to see you thus far on the road to safety, but my own honour demands that I die in battle rather than flee in shame. Fare you well.' And he turned his steed, couched his lance, and rode swiftly and alone into the press of the foe crying 'Argentine, Argentine!' He tried to fight his way towards Sir Edward Bruce, but was borne down by the spears of the schiltrom and slain. The death of this brave knight was mourned by the Scots as well as the English, for he was one of the first three knights of his time and had thrice fought the Saracens, and won great glory by many a feat of arms. He deserved a better fate, but the Scots reverently honoured his noble death, which the leaders could not have prevented.

Now that Sir Aymer and King Edward had fled from the field, the English had nothing left to fight for, and they scattered on every side. The Scots pursued them like furies, and the rout became such a panic-stricken flight that men fell into the swamps and burns, the Bannock burn itself being so jam-packed with bodies of men and horses that men could walk dry-shod over it from bank to bank. The pent-up ire of the common people of Scotland found outlet here, for the small folk ran hither and thither over the field, mercilessly slaying the helpless wounded and dying. Terrible is the anger of the people, though the heart blenches with pity at the thought of such deeds. I have never heard of any army anywhere in such plight as the English were now. If they sought to flee, they drowned, and if they stayed they were slaughtered. Many of them did manage to escape the terrible wrath of the Scots, however, and slink back to England.

King Edward and those who fled with him to Stirling Castle were refused entry by Sir Philip Mowbray, who told them that, for their own sakes, they should ride round to Berwick, for if they came into the castle they would be besieged and surely starved into surrender. He advised them to keep close together, for they would thus be strong enough to hold off any stray party of pursuers.

His advice was taken, and they rode round the New Park, and back to

Linlithgow, whence they kept on for the borders. Douglas had asked Bruce for permission to pursue them, and took sixty men in pursuit, but they were too few to capture the King or face the whole company of English knights in pitched battle. They therefore contented themselves with hanging on their tail and speeding them forth of Scotland. The King himself shipped aboard a boat at Dunbar and was carried by sea to Bamborough. The others got to Berwick, closely harried by Douglas, who picked up more than one straying knight as prisoner on the way, and so into England. Thus King Edward, who had ridden so proudly into Scotland with the greatest army that had yet taken the field, was a few days later glad to escape like a slave by ship, with only a few men about him.

It is said that about half the English army was slain at the battle of Bannockburn, while of the remainder many prisoners were taken. Sir Humphrey de Bohun, Earl of Hereford, escaped with a large army, having simply deserted, and got into Bothwell Castle, still in the hands of the English, with fifty of his retainers. The others rode on to England, but many, it is said, were slain on the way. Many other English knights escaped with part of their army, but so many fled to Stirling Castle, putting their faith in its impregnability, that the rocks about the castle were dotted all over with them, and Bruce was forced to keep his own army vigilant and intact lest they should try to rally and re-attack. The Scots took such a vast haul of war-spoil from the battlefield that many a man made a fortune that way. Bruce eventually attacked Stirling Castle itself, but the weary survivors of the battle made no resistance and were taken prisoner.

The Scots too lost many valiant knights and men, among them Sir Walter Ross, a dear friend of Sir Edward Bruce, who was so cut up by his death that he said he almost wished the battle had been lost rather than Sir Walter killed. This was because Ross was the brother of Sir Edward's dearly loved mistress, for he had come to loathe his own wife, Dame Isobel. This latter fact was the cause of one of the nasty setbacks of the battle, for his brother-in-law, the Earl of Atholl, because of the insult to his sister, raided the Scots supply depot at Cambuskenneth, north of the Forth, and killed the keeper, Sir William Airth, and many of his men. Atholl was later banished to England for this deed and all his lands forfeited to the King.

The Scots were in merry mood after their victory, thankful to God for the grace which had been granted their long struggle under terrible oppression and through great hardship and suffering. The one thing that marred the victory for the King was that Gilbert of Clare, Earl of Gloucester, who had sent Bruce the warning pair of spurs at the court of Edward I when Comyn betrayed him, was found among the slain. The King had his body carried to church and watched over all night before an honourable burial.

Certain English knights surrendered themselves to the King, among them Sir Marmaduke de Twenge, who was in hiding and came forth unarmed to greet the King as he passed. Bruce knew him well, received his surrender, and after courteous treatment he was entertained in a friendly manner and sent home to England ransom-free and with rich gifts from the King. Sir Philip Mowbray also surrendered to the King, and Stirling Castle with him. Sir Philip had honoured his covenant, and the King received him into his peace and his personal household, where he served faithfully to the end of his days.

Great was the turn of Fortune's Wheel that day, for as King Edward went down, the Bruce rose, and many of their retainers with them. Thus ever it is with Fortune, who rules all things beneath the moon, and the turn of whose wheel no man can withstand.

From Stirling, Bruce issued orders that all nobles of both sides killed in battle were to be honourably buried in hallowed ground, and the commonalty given Christian burial in mass graves. Then the towers and castle were mined and razed to the ground. Sir Edward Bruce was sent to besiege Bothwell Castle, where the Earl of Hereford was still lying in the castle, and he persuaded the keeper, Sir Walter Gilbertson, to surrender. The castle thus fell into the hands of Sir Edward Bruce, and all that were in it. The Earl of Hereford was sent to the King as his prisoner. The King sent him back to England, not on the usual ransom basis, but in exchange for the return to Scotland of his wife and daughter and the good Bishop Robert Wishart of Glasgow who had helped crown Bruce King of Scots at Scone. The old man was now blind, and deeply Scotland was in his debt. When the Queen returned with her daughter, Lady Marjory Bruce was betrothed and married to Walter Stewart, and bore him a son Robert. This Robert succeeded Bruce's son (as yet unborn), David II, as King of Scotland, so founding the rule of the House of Stewart, in the lifetime of the present writer, John Barbour.

At the time of the compiling of this book this Robert II has been five years on the throne – the year is now 1375, sixty-one years since the great battle fought at Bannock, and the King is now sixty years old. It is forty-six years since the good King Robert died. May God grant that all Scotsmen will preserve their country and the national integrity of its people, maintaining loyalty and right, as well as did the Bruce in his day!

After Bannockburn King Robert and his people prospered daily, the people grew rich, the country great and strong, the land full of cattle and sheep and corn and such, and all manner of wealth. It was a time of joy and comfort for all the people, of social happiness after great tribulation. King Robert ruled as constitutional monarch, subject to the consent of his people, and advised by his privy council of the Estates. He passed a great deal of valuable legislation, among the first being a law that each and every landlord should come forward within a year and claim his land, showing cause, and doing homage to the King for it. Thus the King, on behalf of the people, brought all lands under the rule and ownership of the nation. And the King raised another army and punished the English for their years of oppression in Scotland by raiding and harrying the whole of the north of England, to make good the immense loss to Scotland caused by the English occupation. But these raids were merely punitive and do not represent any chivalrous achievement. They helped to fill up the aching holes in the Scottish coffers left by English depredation, that is all.

After Bannockburn

I DO not propose to follow in detail the events in which the Bruces were engaged after Bannockburn. The King went on consolidating his rule in Scotland and in strengthening and securing the country. In the period from 1314 to his death in 1328 the great general gradually transformed himself into almost as great a statesman. The chief problem he was confronted with in this period was to establish the kingdom on such authority that, after his death, his work could not easily be undone. The key to this treasure lay in Rome. The Pope had never quite recognised the independence of Scotland because the English exerted pressure on him to refuse to recognise it, and were powerful enough to make their influence felt. The chief preoccupation of King Robert's reign after Bannockburn, therefore, was a long diplomatic battle for Papal recognition, and this he fought with the same infinite patience and dogged skill as he had previously fought his physical campaign against the English. His efforts were crowned with success in 1328, the year before his death, when the Pope gave in and Scotland was fully recognised. This meant that the only international authority, recognised by the whole of Christian Europe, had finally admitted that Scotland was an independent kingdom in its own right; and that recognition, once achieved, could never be undone. This was a greater triumph for King Robert, though less spectacular, than Bannockburn itself.

But if the chief problem confronting the King was the winning of Papal recognition for the kingdom, there was much else besides, of a more mundane sort. Sir Edward Bruce, the King's impetuous and noble brother, decided that Scotland was too small to hold two such men as his brother and himself, so he announced that he intended to make a kingdom for himself in Ireland, which was at this time also under the oppression of the English. Now this decision seems very arbitrary to our eyes, but it is not so pretentious in fact. Ireland and Scotland have a very close connection, for the Scots who eventually gave their name to the whole country originally came from Ulster, and St. Columba of Iona, the chief founding-father of the Scottish Church, was an Irishman. In his time the two Scots kingdoms of Ireland and Dalriada (Argyll) were known simply as the east and the west kingdoms of Scots – Alba and Eire. It was only from about the ninth century on that the terrible scourge of the Norse raids and invasions drove a wedge between the two kingdoms, separating them for a time, perhaps for all time. But it was natural that kings of Scotland should look to Ireland as a family relation, that Scotland and Ireland should help each other against their oppressors, and that Ulstermen should look to the Scottish royal house for a king of their own. Ulster had in fact helped King Robert considerably with smuggled supplies during his long guerilla campaign, and there were times when this Irish help was crucial. Therefore, whatever legal title to the kingship of Ulster, or all Ireland, Sir Edward Bruce might have had, it is not really surprising that the men of Ulster should now invite this proved and highly successful warrior and his kingly brother to help them shake off the yoke of the English in Ireland as they had done in Scotland.

But as this book is about King Robert and his establishment of the Scottish people for all time as an independent nation, I shall not say much about Sir Edward's campaign in Ulster. He succeeded in driving the English out of Ulster and making himself King, then went on to set his rule over the whole of Ireland, but was eventually killed owing to his own ungovernable impetuosity. Ireland suffered by his death, but such a man was made for the saddle rather than the throne and what sort of king in peacetime he would have made is doubtful. He was not, like his brother Robert, as much a statesman as a soldier.

There is one tale, however, of the Irish campaign which does concern us here, for it is about King Robert. The King had subdued the Isles, bringing all the chiefs into his peace except John of Lorne, his implacable enemy. Lorne was eventually captured, but although he refused to submit to the King when brought before him, the Bruce spared his life and had him sent to Loch Leven, where he ended his days on the island in the loch. Scotland now at peace, the King went to help his brother in Ireland, leaving Walter Stewart and James Douglas to guard Scotland in his absence.

The Scots had subdued all the north of Ireland, and the King of Scotland was campaigning on behalf of his brother near Limerick, in the south. They had rested for a few days there, and were just preparing to march off again, after considerable trouble of preparations, when the King heard a woman scream. He at once sent a man to find out what had happened. When he came back, he said, 'Sire, it is one of the laundry-women who has just gone into labour-pains for the birth of her child. We cannot take her with us, and will have to leave her here. It is this fear as much as the pain that makes her cry so.'

'No wonder,' said the King, 'and what kind of men would we be if we rode off and left a woman in such straits? We would insult the women who bore us. We will stay here until the child has been born.'

The King not only held up his whole army, but had a tent unpacked and pitched, and the woman brought into it. Then he had other women of the camp attend her, and gave orders that she be carried on a litter by the army when it moved off. And people were greatly touched by this courtesy to a poor laundress by so great a king. Yet they need not have been, for it is precisely the great men who are great in apparently small things as well as large.

But in Scotland there was still a good deal of trouble along the borders with England, and the good Sir James had many a dangerous battle on his hands. There was one castle still in English hands, the castle of Berwick, and it was a constant source of trouble to the Scots, Douglas in particular, until it was taken in a manner I shall presently describe. Douglas became a name of terror to the English, and it is said that women used to use his name to subdue their children as if it were the Devil's.

In 1324 a son, David, was born to the King, and this son became David II of Scotland. King Edward II of England made one last attempt to regain power in Scotland, but the Scots so met him with their scorched-earth policy that nothing could be found for his men to eat when they invaded. After one such foray only one solitary, skinny cow was produced, which caused an English knight to comment, 'There goes the dearest beef I ever saw, for it must have cost us at least a thousand pounds!' King Robert, ever seeking to put the kingdom out of reach of danger, proposed a marriage between his baby son and the Princess Joanna of England, and this led to the Treaty of Northampton in 1328, by which the English at last acknowledged the independence of the Scottish kingdom. This was followed by the Papal bull permitting the Scots King to be anointed and crowned, which meant that Rome too acknowledged the independence of the kingdom. Prince David was in fact anointed and crowned, thereby mounting a stronger throne than any Scottish King had ever known. This was the consummation of the Bruce's work for Scotland.

But there were troubles, too, in plenty still in Scotland, among them a treacherous plot against the King's life. King Robert created many enemies for himself by his policy of seizing the lands of those nobles who were traitors to him, and handing them over to his own men. He consolidated friendships by this means, but he also created a pack of disinherited exiles who schemed and constantly plotted against him and his, and this legacy lived on to plague the King's successors long after he was dead. Some such now plotted to assassinate him, but they were discovered in time and the King executed on them the terrible sentence for treason invented by his old opponent, Edward I – he had them hanged and disembowelled. This cruelty estranged some men from him, including Ingram de Umphraville, who had come into the King's peace, like Sir Philip Mowbray and others who had fought against Bruce until the battle of Bannockburn.

The most important and significant event of this period, however, happened in 1320. The struggle between Bruce and the Pope for recognition of the independence of the kingdom was at its most intense, and Pope John XXII was proving to be an enemy of Scotland, and supporter of the pretensions of Edward II of England. The weapon of excommunication was wielded gainst the Scots, not for the first time since the fight for independence had begun. It was double-edged, for it proved that the Scots could safely ignore it, though not without cost, and the Pope simply weakened his authority by using this spiritual sanction in the despicable political cause of Edward. The four leading Scottish bishops were excommunicated in this cause, and as a result the barons of Scotland, who called themselves, along with all other men of influence and power, 'the community of the realm', sent a letter to the Pope. This letter seems to have been drafted by Bernard of Linton, who was abbot of Arbroath, and chancellor to King Robert. It was sent round all the men of property in Scotland, and most of these appended their seals to it, to show their approval. The letter, which must have been the product of much discussion among the signatories, or the foremost of them, is a great document. It is too long to quote here, but part of it ought to be known by heart by every Scotsman:

'Our nation lived in freedom and peace, until that august prince, Edward, King of England, the father of the present King, finding our realm without a king, and our people innocent of evil intent and still unused to the assaults of war, came to us in the guise of a friend and ally and then made a hostile attack upon us. As for the wrongs he inflicted upon us – the slaughter, violence, pillage, conflagration, prelates imprisoned, monasteries burned down and their inmates robbed and slain, and all the other outrages which he perpetrated on our people, sparing neither age nor sex nor religious order – none could describe nor even conceive these things unless he had actually experienced them.

'From these innumerable evils, with the aid of Him who woundeth and His hands make whole, we have been delivered by our most valiant Prince and King, Robert; who, that he might free his people and heritage from the hands of the enemy, rose like another Joshua or Maccabeus, and cheerfully endured toil and weariness, hunger and peril. He it is that by the providence of God we have made our Prince and King, not only by right of succession according to our laws and customs, which we are resolved to maintain unto the death, but also with the due consent and assent of us all. Unto him, by whom salvation has been wrought unto our people, we are bound for the preservation of our liberties, both by force of law and out of gratitude for all he has done; and unto him we are determined in all things to adhere. But were he to abandon the task to which he has set his hand or to show any disposition to subject us or our realm to the King of England or the English, we would instantly strive to expel him as our enemy and the betrayer of his own rights and ours, and we would choose another King to rule over us who would be equal to the task of our defence.

'For so long as one hundred men remain alive, we shall never under any conditions submit to the domination of the English. It is not for glory or riches or honours that we fight, but only for liberty, which no good man will consent to lose but with his life.'

This document establishes once and for all the sovereignty of the Scottish people as a nation over king, crown, church, state, and any power whatsoever under only God, and the right and determination of the people to assert that sovereignty over against any king, state, church, or any power whatsoever that dares to challenge it. For the rights of the people are held from God alone and by no human intermediacy whatsoever.

It is ironical that some of the signatories were arraigned for treason that same year: but it is clear from the above that it was to Scotland and not to Robert Bruce that the signatories owed their allegiance.

The Capture and Holding of Berwick

ALL Scotland after Bannockburn was now under King Robert's rule except Berwick, where the English continued to hold out and make a nuisance of themselves to Douglas and the border men until 1318. In that year it was taken by the combined forces of Randolph and Douglas, with the help of a Berwick townsman.

There was a man called Sym of Spalding living in Berwick, and he found the English oppression more and more intolerable. At last he got in touch with one of the Scots leaders to whom he was related by marriage, and offered to help the Scots take the town by stratagem. The message was conveyed directly to the King, because rivalry had broken out between Randolph and Douglas, and to help the one was to offend the other. The King therefore arranged that both men should take Berwick and share the glory of its capture, and they met one night and, guided by Sym of Spalding, climbed unguarded bits of the wall by ladders, and were hidden by Sym till dawn. But the rivalry between the two factions was so great that both sides broke the plan and began to raid the town before due time, pillaging and slaying as if they were madmen. Despite this indiscipline they did manage to take the town, though a number of the English escaped into the castle, which was still untaken.

About noon, when the Scots were thoroughly in command of the town, and rather unguardedly making the most of their chances, the English garrison in the castle saw the Scottish standard carelessly guarded. Suddenly they opened their gates and a troop of well-armed men rode out to the attack. The Scots were taken by surprise and in poor order, and things would have gone very badly with them indeed had not a certain new knight, Sir William of Keith and Galston, saved the day by his brilliant and vigorous leadership, and the English were driven back into the castle with great loss of men.

Now that the town was taken, though with some discreditable behaviour on the part of the Scots, it was only a matter of time before the castle too must fall. Word was sent to the King that the town was now his, and Bruce set out at once with an army to besiege the castle, greatly pleased that the last English outpost in Scotland had been rescued by the Scots. But when the English garrison in the castle saw the strength of the Scots arrayed against them, and the obvious hopelessness of their case, they surrendered the castle, about five days after the taking of the town. They were allowed to go in peace back to their own country, and when the King arrived he found the whole of Berwick, castle included, already in Scottish hands.

The King decided to preserve and garrison the castle, keeping both town and it well stocked as a frontier-post, and young Walter the Steward was given wardenship of the place. The King and his army went foraying in the north of England and brought back great abundance of cattle and other valuables, and left both town and castle with at least a year's supplies, in case of siege. Walter the Steward gathered a powerful garrison about him, some 500 veterans and sundry archers and cross-bowmen from among the local people. He had also with him a certain Fleming called John Crab, an engineer of great skill and ingenuity, who began at once to fortify the castle against attack, setting up engines, cranes, producing Greek fire, and all manner of other things used in defence. There was no cannon at that time in Scotland.

Having seen the town thus garrisoned against English reprisal, the noble King left again for Lothian, leaving Walter in charge.

King Edward of England was furious when he heard of the fall of Berwick, and at once summoned a council of war, and prepared to lead an army to besiege the town. He planned to dig trenches and set his army in them so that, if the Scots came to relieve the besieged town, they would find the English army so strongly entrenched that it would be almost invulnerable to attack. And he marched with a mighty army including the flower of England's chivalry, the saintly Sir Thomas of Lancaster among them. He also ordered his navy to bring up various supplies by sea, so that they should not be caught out by the Scots policy of scorched-earth.

With this great host King Edward settled in at Berwick, appointing one of his great lords over each of the quartering-fields, and soon there was a greater town of tents and pavilions there than the whole township of Berwick itself, while English ships filled the harbour and the sea outside it. The Scots inside the town prepared themselves to fight to the death. Most of the fighting-men were of the same clan as Walter Stewart, their gracious captain, men of high courage and determination, and unswerving loyalty to him.

Six days passed without any real fighting between the two sides, while the English dug their fortified trenches round their encampment. But having done so, they turned their full attentions to attacking the township, and on the eve of the Nativity of the Virgin, they came against the defenders with scaling-gear and all sorts of engines for besieging strong walls.

The Scots manned their appointed places on the walls and waited the enemy. When all was ready on the English side, the trumpets were sounded and the assault began. Each battlement of the walls was attacked by a party of English archers, and matched by archers on the battlements themselves. Infantrymen rushed forward with long scaling-ladders which they hurriedly tried to swarm up, while the defenders made every effort to throw them down. The truth is that the walls were too low, being only about fourteen feet or so in height, and the defenders were hard pressed. Walter Stewart himself rode about the place with a company of horse, sending help where it was most needed, ceaselessly checking up on the course of the struggle at all points, and in general showing himself a worthy pupil of King Robert, his father-in-law. The English completely surrounded the town, so it was no easy task to keep in touch with the battle at all points.

The battle raged until afternoon without any decisive gains on either side. Then the English in the ships rigged out one of their ships as an assault tower, with a bridge to stretch from the mast to the walls of the town and a tower and platform for men to surge up and cross it. This ship, full of well-armed men, they manœuvred in towards the walls, past the bridge-house, until they got her very near indeed, so that the defenders could see the bustling men scurrying about on her. A hail of arrows, stones and cross-bolts, and other artillery met its approach, so that they could not get her close enough to drop the bridge. But the men on board fought hard as long as the tide was with them, and indeed so far forgot their seamanship, those who had it, that they forgot the tide altogether and the ship was left grounded by the ebbing water. This was a fatal mistake, for as soon as the defenders saw what had happened, they sallied out from the gates and set fire to her. The whole ship went up in flames and many on board were slain as they tried to flee. The Scots captured the famous engineer who had been responsible for the ship's fitting out and general plan, and returned to the town. They were lucky to get back behind closed gates before a huge company of the English arrived, attracted by the fire, with great speed. But the gates were safely barred in time.

The battle raged thus all day, and by evening it was clear to the English they that had lost the day, and the retreat was sounded. They were exhausted and many were seriously wounded or dead. Those inside were in no better case, and both sides were glad of a respite. It was another five days before the English felt rested enough to make another assault.

Meanwhile King Robert had learned of the siege, and he at once gathered an army to go to its relief. But the King knew that the English were entrenched, and judged it unwise to make a frontal assault on their trenches. So he thought up a plan to counter this move of King Edward's. He sent Randolph and Douglas with a large army into the north of England to burn and slay and generally spread havoc there, so that when the besiegers of Berwick heard of this, their morale was undermined with worry for their own homes and people, and for their goods. Douglas and Randolph mercilessly harried the whole of the north as far as Ripon, which they utterly destroyed, and camped at Boroughbridge and Mitton close by. But the English of the district got together a large army, headed by the Archbishop of York, and prepared to do battle with the Scots. It was only a citizen army, but it far outnumbered the Scots war-party, and when the hardy Scottish veterans formed into two battalions under Douglas and Randolph and advanced to meet them, the English came confidently on. They marched so close that the English and Scots could see the colour of each other's eyes, barely three spear-lengths apart: then suddenly the English panicked and fled. Unfortunately for them it was too late before they grasped the difference between their fighting qualities and their grim, war-hardened opponents. The Scots fell upon them with their habitual ferocity and mercilessly slew huge numbers, it is said even 300 priests among them. They reaped the blacksmith work of Edward I, the boasted 'Hammer of the Scots', for he had hammered the Scots into the hardiest, steel-tempered army in Europe. So much for hammers. And because of the slaughter of priests there, this skirmish was known as 'the Chapter of Mitton'. After it, the Scots marched on through the north of England, laying waste and death and destruction wherever they went, while the English army lay fretting at Berwick.

Before the fifth day had passed, the English at Berwick had made various engines for a renewed attack. Among other contraptions they made a great 'sow', a sort of shelter with a hard roof to protect a platoon of men from attack from above, various mining tools to get under the walls, scaffolds and towers higher than the walls of the town, and the like. They also prepared an attack by sea.

The defenders, seeing such preparation of engines of destruction, set up, under the guidance of Crab the Fleming, a high derrick on wheels, so that it could be moved about the battlements wherever needed. They also took tar and pitch and lint and hards, brimstone and dry sticks that would burn easily, and of these materials made great faggots which they bound up with bands of iron, as many of them as filled a huge tun. These they intended to use against the sow if it came against the wall, dropping the flaming bundles from the derrick, at the same time pinioning the contraption with grappling chains so that it could not be freed from the area of fire. They also made slings for throwing great stones, and had every man well briefed in his line and place of duty. Sir Walter Stewart rode bravely about with armed men, keeping a vigilant eye on how things were going, and rushing in to help wherever he saw most need.

Both sides having thus prepared for the attack, the English army blew their trumpets for the attack at dawn of Rood Eve. Then they came on with their many engines of assault, quickly surrounded the town and attacked it strongly, putting hard pressure on the garrison. The Scots for their part put up a good defence, exposing themselves fearlessly to wounds and violent death. Ladders run up against the walls were thrust off by long poles and sent crashing to the ground; stones catapulted powerfully against foes so that many fell dead or wounded. English foot soldiery swiftly withdrew these wounded, returning swiftly to continuous attack. Mightily the Scots defenders laboured to repel them, wounding so many with such constant exertion that backward the onset slowly was driven.

Thus till near noon hardily they contested. Then the besiegers brought up their engine, the great sow with men in it, flanked by troops in armour, and trundled it up to the walls. The defenders at once produced the English engineer they had captured on the ship and swore to put him to death unless he showed them how to destroy the engine. Seeing that he had no choice, this man ordered the catapult to be loaded with a huge rock, and himself aimed and fired it. It barely missed the sow, passing over it and falling a little bit behind it. Again the engineer had her loaded and took aim. Out swished the stone with a whirring noise, like the wings of some great bird, and fell right in front of the sow. The morale of the men inside it was being sapped by these terrifying whirrings and ground-shaking thuds. A third time the catapult was bent and out swished the stone, high in the air, then the great heaviness dived deadly down with furious whirring force and crashed right on top of the engine, shattering the main beam and rafters in flying splinters and sending it crashing to the ground. Men were seen crawling out from under it amid groans and grunts and screams of the wounded; and the watching, jubilant defenders shouted, 'Look, the great sow has farrowed!'

John Crab then brought up his ready gear, fired his faggots and hurled them over the wall on to the sow, burning it to charred cinders.

Meantime the English main army was attacking on all sides, while the Scots fought back manfully and at great risk of life and limb in defence. The English navy threw in ships to the assault, each rigged out with mighty engines of war, their topcastles crammed with men in armour, and their lifeboats drawn up and fastened high upon their masts. One sailed right up under the wall but the English engineer working for the Scots trained his catapult on her and stove in a longboat filled with men up on the mast, spilling the men head over heels dead or stunned upon the deck. After that the ships were afraid to come within range.

The main attack by land was so very fierce that it is a wonder the Scots managed to hold it at all. They were at a great disadvantage, as I've said, because of the lowness of the walls, the defenders' faces being within reach of a spear thrust. Many were indeed sorely wounded thus, and the rest were kept so busy that none had time to rest. Their enemies battered them so strongly that their leader, riding about with his company of horse, often came upon places where the defenders were all dead or wounded, and had to leave some of his own men there to hold the wall. By the time he had made one complete round of the walls he had only one man left with him.

The English force attacking the Marygate hacked the barrier down and set fire to the drawbridge, gathering in great numbers at the gate itself, to burn it down. Word was sent to Sir Walter at once of the grave danger here, and he called out the reserves in the castle itself, as yet unattacked that day, and hurried to the spot. He saw the peril at once, and determined on a bold stroke, perhaps attributable to his apprenticeship to the good Sir James. He had the gate thrown wide open and sallied out with his men, scattering the English and putting out the already lit fires. There followed a ferocious skirmish of grim in-fighting as the English surged back on the defenders, all were stabbing, thrusting, slashing, the groans and grunts of the wounded mingling with the swishing and thudding of the blows. But the Scots held the gate till night fell, causing both sides to retreat. The English withdrew in a state of exhaustion, having been badly savaged, and tried to get some rest in their quarters, with only a few men appointed to keep watch.

It was a critical night for all of them, the English marvelling at the stoutness of the defence, the Scots heartened by their success. They had lost but few men, but many were sorely wounded, and all utterly exhausted. It had been an assault so desperate that I have never heard of so few men make better defence against so many. At the height of the attack, the women and children inside the walls helped the defenders by gathering up arrows and carrying them in armfuls to the men on the walls – yet not one was killed or wounded.

The night passed quietly enough, but in the morning the English got news of the havoc wrought by Bruce's army at Boroughbridge and Mitton, and the harrying of the whole of the north of England. And when Edward heard this news, he called a council of war to decide whether they should continue the siege or march against the Scots in England. This council was divided, the men of the north naturally, fearing for their own goods and people, voting for immediate action against the Scots, the men of the south, having nothing to lose, wanting to carry on the siege. Thus Bruce once again had weakened, divided, and undermined his enemies by indirect methods. The quarrel was so severe that, when King Edward decided in favour of the southern faction, Earl Thomas of Lancaster deserted with his whole army. This led to his being hanged, beheaded, and drawn for treason later on, and many of his men with him, at Pontefract. But Earl Thomas's defection decided the issue, for Edward had lost a third of his total force, and he had to raise the siege and return to England.

As soon as Randolph and Douglas heard that the plan had worked and the English had left Berwick, they went home to Scotland via Carlisle and the west coast, taking their many prisoners and much plunder with them. The King was in jubilant mood, for he had scarcely lost a man, had raised the siege of Berwick without a single confrontation with the English army, and his captains had returned laden with prisoners and spoil. The tales of the victors so rejoiced him that he ordered games and entertainments in their honour.

Thus Bruce demonstrated once again that the best way to fight an enemy is not to confront him where he is most prepared, but to counter-attack where he least expects it and is most vulnerable. The strategy was a variation of the well-known one of attacking from the rear as well as from the front, in a pincer movement, dividing the enemy by forcing him to fight on two fronts at once.

The King rode to Berwick himself and had all the details of the siege and defence pointed out to him. He was intensely interested in these details and greatly praised the action of the defenders, and in particular Walter Stewart's daring action at the Marygate, which undoubtedly was the crisis of the whole action. And the King stayed for some time at Berwick, ordering, before he left, that the walls should be built ten feet higher all round the town and sending far and wide for masons to do this work.

The Death of King Robert

PEACE was at last achieved in Scotland; the Treaty of Northampton of 1328 ended the English claim to sovereignty over the country; a bull from the Pope granting the Scots the right to anoint and crown their kings, the final proof of the independence of the kingdom, was on the way; and the proposed marriage of Prince David Bruce to Princess Joanna Plantagenet of England promised not only peace but friendship between the two countries. The work of the greatest of all Scottish kings was done, and he might now have enjoyed the old age of peace and fulfilment he had so wonderfully earned. But alas, no man is master of his own fate, and about this time an old illness which the King had contracted in the days of his outlawry, caused by the hardship and conditions under which he had to live, lying out of doors at night in all weathers, returned.

This illness prevented the King attending the marriage of his son, but he sent Randolph and Douglas to Berwick to meet the young princess, who came north with her mother and Mortimer. There the young couple were married, while the King lay, semi-paralysed, for so his illness afflicted him, at Cardross. He did not see the revelry of both Scots and English in that place of Berwick where they had so recently fought such grim warfare; nor the feasting which went on for many a day without cross word between Scots and English, who were now learning that mutual respect for each other's independence is the only ground of true neighbourliness, each willing the good of the other instead of trying to dominate. After this feasting and enjoyment, the Queen returned to England, and Randolph and Douglas brought the young and beautiful English princess (for indeed she became the fairest of her time) home to her husband's house in Scotland, and to the ailing King, who welcomed them both.

The King, far-sighted as ever, and knowing his death was upon him, caused a parliament to be called, and set before his people his plan to crown his son and the young queen in his own, King Robert's, lifetime. The parliament consented, and the young king and queen were crowned, the king being the first to be crowned and anointed by the authority of the Pope. This fact was Bruce's greatest achievement, and the seal on his life's work, for it made Scotland for ever an independent and sovereign kingdom, internationally and universally recognised as such. And before the coronation, King Robert caused an ordinance to be passed that declared, in the event of the Prince David dying without a male heir of his own, the succession should go to the King's grandson, Robert Stewart, son of Marjory Bruce and Walter Stewart. All the lords swore an oath on this succession, and put their seals to it. And the King also ordained that, if he himself were to die during the minority of his son David, Randolph and Douglas were to be regents until King David came of age. These two lords swore to this, the nobles agreeing and swearing faithfully to obey them loyally if such an eventuality happened.

When all these matters had been attended to, the King retired again to Cardross, where his illness steadily worsened, and he knew the time had come for him to face the end of all human existence. He sent for the chief men of the country, and when they came, he told them his last will and testament. He gave a lot of money to various religious bodies for the salvation of his soul, among other bequests, and then addressed his lords:

'Gentlemen,' he said, 'my day is far spent and the only thing left for me to do now is to meet death fearlessly, as every man must. I thank God that He has granted me time enough to make my confession and seek grace at my end. I am acutely aware of the fact that my decision to take up the cause of Scottish independence has resulted in much shedding of blood, and many innocent people have suffered and been slain. Let this last pain of mine be my penance for my share of the guilt in that sin, and for all ways ever I offended. I have one last desire, though, which weighs heavily upon me. My heart was determined that, as penance for the slaying of Comyn in a church, I should make a crusade against God's enemies as soon as I could properly free myself from the cares of Scotland to consider my own salvation. Now that this time has come, my work in Scotland almost completed, I no longer have the strength of body to fulfil that other, personal purpose. The salvation of my country has left me no strength to do much about my own salvation, and that grieves me. Therefore, since my heart wills what my body cannot achieve, my last wish is that my heart should go where I cannot follow it, to fight the Saracens. I beg you, gentlemen, to comply with this wish of mine and choose one of yourselves, a knight honest, wise, and mighty in battle, a noble man of his hands, to carry my heart against the enemies of God when my body and soul have been severed for ever. I want a man worthy of this task, who will be to my heart as my own body was, valiant and true.'

At these words many a strong man broke down and wept, indeed none could stifle their grief at the hearing. For rarely have a people owed so much to one man, rarely could a man less be spared to pay his human account, and bleak was the future that spread before their eyes, when Bruce should be taken from them. But the King motioned them to control their grief, saying it could not really help them and would only increase their own pain. And he charged them again to consider his wish. Then they all conferred among themselves, and decided that the best man for the task was the good Sir James Douglas, and they told the King so. The King was pleased and said, 'As I hope to be saved, I am very pleased by your decision, for he was my own choice, and I value no man higher. But let us find out what he himself thinks.'

A man was sent to summon Douglas into the King's presence, and when he came, the King told him what was in his mind. And Douglas knelt beside the royal death-bed and, bowing his head, said, 'Sire, I find it difficult to express my thanks for your many great benefits freely given me so often since I first came into your service. But for this great honour you now do me I am grateful above all others, that you should give into my keeping your most noble, illustrious and valorous heart. What can I say but that I will gladly undertake this mission for you, and in all ways fulfil your wishes, if God gives me but time enough to do it.' The dying King took Douglas's hand in both of his and with uninhibited emotion tenderly thanked him. And there was not a dry eye in all that company looking on.

The King grew gradually weaker and weaker, the last rites were said over him, and he gave up the ghost as a true Christian should, and who can doubt that God took him to Himself in heaven, to be among the chosen and the choiring angels. And when the people learned of the death of King Robert, terrible was the wail of lamentation that went up throughout the land. Men were to be seen tearing their hair, the toughest knights were unashamed to weep and wring their hands, to rend their clothes like madmen, for they knew that never again would they benefit from such nobleness, wisdom, strength, honesty, and above all, such courteous companionship. And they lamented him thus:

'Alas, now all our security and peace will end with him who has been our comfort, our wisdom, our guide and commander. His valour alone, his mighty strength, made all around him valorous and strong, so that none could be dismayed while he was with them. What more can we do or say? He was the saviour of his country, and while he lived all our foes feared and respected us, and our fame and valour with his was spread far and wide. All this we owe to him alone.'

Thus they mourned, as no ruler was ever mourned, and with good reason, for there was but one such Robert Bruce. But even in this sorrow, those nearest the King honoured his last desire. They disembowelled him and took the heart from his body, and gave it to Sir James Douglas. The body was then richly embalmed and buried with all ceremony of state in Dunfermline Abbey, in a splendid tomb in the choir there. And Douglas had the heart of Bruce put into a silver casket and hung it about his neck, never putting it off. Then he put his own affairs in order, made his will and testament, left orders for the governing of his lands, all with wise and thorough foresight. Then he shipped from Berwick with a company of knights and sailed to Seville in Spain, where they landed after a stormy voyage.

Douglas was well received at the court of the King of Spain, and offered rich gifts of gold and gear, all of which he refused, saying that he was on a pilgrimage against God's enemies, and as the reward he sought was for his soul in heaven it would be unbecoming to accept worldly reward, and that all he desired of the King of Spain was to be allowed to help him in his fight against the Saracens. The King was greatly impressed by this answer, and put Douglas in the care of men highly experienced in war against the Saracens. And knights came from all quarters to see the famous Scottish knight, and especially among them were many English knights, who greatly honoured him.

Among these knights was one who had the reputation of being the doughtiest in all Christendom. His face was so scarred by wounds that there was scarcely an inch of it unscarred. And when this man saw Douglas, who had not a single mark on his face, he asked how could so famous a knight still have the unscarred face of a boy. Douglas looked at him and said, very quietly, 'I have always been blessed with hands to guard my face.' And the knights around him looked at him with renewed respect.

Very soon Douglas went into battle against the Saracen king of Belmarine, and in the hard fighting followed this procedure: first he threw the heart of Bruce ahead of him, as far as he could, then fought his way through to it and picked it up again. Then he threw it ahead again, and again followed it, picked it up and threw it on. At first all went well, and the Christian side won the fighting. But the Saracens rallied and attacked again, and in this second part of the battle Douglas and others went to the aid of Sir William St. Clair, who was sorely pressed, and they were all slain – Douglas, Sir William, and the Logans.

Thus died the good Sir James Douglas bearing the heart of King Robert the Bruce into battle against the Saracens, and great was the mourning among his own men. And they searched the field after the battle and found the heart of King Robert, still in its silver casket, and brought it home to Scotland. They could not take the body of Sir James with them, but they disembowelled him and boiled the flesh from the bones, burying it reverently in holy ground in Spain: the bones they brought back to Scotland along with the heart of the King.

There these tales end. Randolph governed Scotland well for many a year until he met his death by poison, and it is said that he died by the hand of his mistress, as is recorded in the ballad of Lord Randal.

May all true Scots do as well by their country as these great forefathers did in their time, taking example by their excellence.

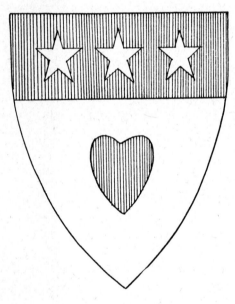

Douglas. After 1330.